Praise for David Taylor's
THE NAKED LEADER

'The business-book bestseller executives are taking on holiday'
Financial Times

'At last – a self-help book that is actually helpful'
Computing

'This book makes success within everyone's grasp'
Daily Mirror

'David provides easy-to-learn, proven methods and skills that produce outstanding results ... If you are into leadership, then you must be into *The Naked Leader*'
René Carayol, co-author of *Corporate Voodoo*

'An extraordinary book for an extraordinary time ... Compulsory reading for any organization that believes in the power of a motivated workforce'
Simon La Fosse, Director, Harvey Nash plc

'Drives a stake through the heart of everything consultants have told us for the last twenty years'
David Oliver, CEO, Nascent Form

'This is the right book, by the right person, at the right time. It changed my life'
Peter Warman, Chairman, Deep-Think

'David has the ability to take the seemingly complex and break it into manageable, understandable and memorable strategies for improvement'
David Butler, Founder and CEO, The Butler Cox Foundation

'The first must-read book of the 21st century, a masterpiece'
Thomas Power, Chairman, Ecademy

'David is the UK's leading light of leadership development'
Michael Gough, Chief Executive, NCC

'At last – th... ... ...tiatives;
there is an...
Robin Bloc...

'A journey of enlightened leadership, lead by the Naked Leader of our time'
Julie Bryant, Creative Director, The Creative Consultancy

'*The Naked Leader* brings fun, adventure and inspiration back into business and personal success'
Adrian Gilpin, Chairman, The Institute of Human Development

'I have bought a copy for my daughters and my whole family – your book is one of the must-read books of all time'
Maurice Spillane, CEO, Appligenics

'*The Naked Leader* does exactly what it says on the "tin"'
Business Plus

'Enlightenment at last – business success through being yourself!'
Dr Alan Rae, Founder, Executive Studio

'Brilliantly written. An antidote to the usual soporific management tomes'
Michael Clarke, Founder, ACTS

'At last! An entertaining business book that really delivers – and about time too!'
Rob Wirszycz, Director, Momentum Capital

'I had been taken hostage by life until I read *The Naked Leader*. It makes pursuing the truth great fun'
Paul Stephenson, CEO and Founder, EGOstream

'*The Naked Leader* uses the most advanced techniques available to transform people's ideas about life, without once resorting to jargon, mystery or academic double-speak'
Joe Crosbie, Head of Marketing, The Children's Society

'*The Naked Leader* shows us not only how to understand ourselves and what we really want, but also what we need to do to achieve it. I strongly recommend this to anyone who wants to achieve their real potential'
Kris Kebby, Systems Director, Royal & Sun Alliance

'I loved the refreshing honesty and truth of *The Naked Leader* and that it contained practical suggestions which I could apply immediately. And its style is wonderful'
Jeff Skinner, Human Resources Director, 3M

'The most powerful book I have ever read (and I've read a few!)'
Vincenza Douglas, Founder and CEO, Something Beginning with V

'*The Naked Leader* inspires, encourages and enlightens . . . This engages everyone, turning dreams into reality'
Wendy Thorley, Head of Information Systems, RSPCA

'David Taylor is not only a genius, but a brave genius, for daring to stand up and take leadership back to the single issue that really matters: YOU'
Tony Dowd, Project Manager, Aon Consulting

'I have successfully applied the principles of Naked Leadership in both my professional and personal life since reading the book; I'd recommend the book to anybody who wishes to make a difference to their life!'
Paul Heath, Leadership Consultant

'*The Naked Leader* is guaranteed to change the way you think and feel about yourself as a leader'
Robin Harris, IT Director, Smith & Nephew

'David has this incredible ability to energize every individual. He helps you to see that your dreams are achievable'
Peter Shuttleworth, Head of Service Management, MoD

'What a breath of fresh air in comparison to all the jargon books out there'
Lewis Cunningham, Project Manager, Cornhill Insurance

'At last, a business book that is fun to read, relevant to everybody and truly life-changing'
Jon Bernstein, Silicon.com

Also by David Taylor

THE NAKED LEADER

and published by Bantam Books

the naked leader experience

david taylor

with love
David x

BANTAM BOOKS

LONDON • NEW YORK • TORONTO • SYDNEY • AUCKLAND

THE NAKED LEADER EXPERIENCE
A BANTAM BOOK : 0 553 81647 0

First publication in Great Britain

PRINTING HISTORY
Bantam edition published 2004

3 5 7 9 10 8 6 4 2

Copyright © David Taylor 2004

Please visit *www.nakedleader.com* for details of David's next book, and to join the
Naked Leader Network.

Set in 10½/14pt Optima by
Falcon Oast Graphic Art Ltd.

Bantam Books are published by Transworld Publishers,
61–63 Uxbridge Road, London W5 5SA,
a division of The Random House Group Ltd,
in Australia by Random House Australia (Pty) Ltd,
20 Alfred Street, Milsons Point, Sydney, NSW 2061, Australia,
in New Zealand by Random House New Zealand Ltd,
18 Poland Road, Glenfield, Auckland 10, New Zealand
and in South Africa by Random House (Pty) Ltd,
Endulini, 5a Jubilee Road, Parktown 2193, South Africa.

Printed and bound in Great Britain by
Cox & Wyman Ltd, Reading, Berkshire.

Papers used by Transworld Publishers are natural, recyclable products made from
wood grown in sustainable forests. The manufacturing processes conform to the
environmental regulations of the country of origin.

www.booksattransworld.co.uk

For my nieces and nephews with love:

Hadley, Howard, Kate, Kelsey, Lucas,
Michael, Nicola, Scott, Thomas and Tracey

ACKNOWLEDGEMENTS

Thank you to those who contributed to this book, who are spreading the message that sets people free, and to the following, who kept me going with their belief, support and inspiration, when it was most needed . . .

For their input throughout this book, I thank you up front in case I forget to mention you elsewhere!

Rosalind (wife and soul-mate), Olivia (without whom this would not be an adventure), The Other Person (who wishes to remain anonymous), Stephen Clint (the most organized person I know), Adrian Gilpin (you taught me that all this stuff must be available to all), Michael Gough (a leader for the twenty-first century), Igor Ledochowski (I could not have written those two chapters without you), Steve Rock (the master storyteller) and Maurice Spillane (a poet, indeed).

Also, massive thank-yous to Brenda Kimber at Bantam (one amazing editor!), and to John Blake for his tireless proofreading.

And love, warmth and thanks to: God, Adam Afriyie, Jonathan Andrews, Tracey Ball, David Barker, Lesley Barker-Smith, Brendan Barnes, Buffy Barrington, Simon Benham, Gareth Brown, Sue Cabot, René Carayol, Frank and Wendy Chapman, Robina Chatham, Phil Clark, Jim Close, Glenn

Cockerill and everyone at Woking FC, Tina Compton, Paul Crittenden, Tricia Davey, Michael Dean, Ken Deeks, Allard de Jong, Guy Dominy, Neale Donald Walsch, Vincenza Douglas, Tricia Drakes, Vanessa Ford, Jerry Foulkes, Steph Harris, Mike Hensman, Delia Hyde, Nicky Jefferies, Kate Jones, Naomi Langford-Wood, Des Lee, Liz Levy, Hugh Macken, Mike Oldfield, Bill Parslow, Nina Parson, Steve Pauley, Brinley Platts, Tony Pybus, Chris and Kevin Redmond, Simon Reina-Shaw, Nigel Risner, Anthony Robbins, Malcolm Rose, Kate Scarles, Laura Sherlock, Jane Short, Lisa Stephen, Julie Thompson, Judy Thomson, Sarah Thornton, Judith Underhill, Tim Wheater, Jill Whittington, Georgina Woudstra, Christopher Young.

All the wonders you seek are within yourself

Thomas Brown

Contents

Book Two
Reignite Your Relationships

Book Three
Reinvent Your Organization

your invitation

Your Personal Invitation To:

The Naked Leader Experience

You are invited to read this book:

Traditionally – As the book is printed
The Author's Choice – In the order the book was written
Or Your Choice – In *any* way, or order that you wish

Required Dress: None

Thank you for reading this far.

No, I kid you not. Over half of business and personal-development books are never even started, so I am very grateful that you have actually read this first paragraph!

We've all been there – standing in the bookshop or searching online. We see THE BOOK that will change our lives for ever. Yes, we already have a vast collection of books that we have not quite managed to read yet, but this time it is going to be different. This time we will find the one, the answer.

A quick glance and we are sold. We have at last found THE BOOK that will ensure we find the perfect partner, lead our people to success, live the life of our dreams, or whatever. We buy it.

Sitting down on the train, we make our first choice – evening paper or THE BOOK? No contest, the paper wins. After all, it's been a long day. We will read THE BOOK later, when we are relaxed.

We arrive home, and place THE BOOK on one side, ready for the grand reading, or at least the start.

We carry THE BOOK upstairs at bedtime and put it next to the bed. During the night it sits there, staring at us, impatiently screaming, READ ME.

Then, sometime later, the book walks, head down, to the shelves to join the other great unreads.

So what will encourage you to keep reading this book? By making it relate to your favourite subject – *You*!

And remember, this book is not my book, it is yours. It will be your experience. What you read in it, choose to take from it, and apply to your life, they are all your decisions, and yours alone.

A key message in this book, and in being a Naked

Leader, is that there are no answers, there are only choices. And the choices you make will shape the rest of your life. Let's start with one of the biggest choices of all. (If you've read *The Naked Leader* this will be a good reminder, if not . . .)

Imagine If . . .

There is a word beginning with 'F' that we unknowingly teach our children from when they are very young. And they grow up very, very attached to it.

It stops us in our tracks, we worry about it day and night and, in many ways, as we grow up, we carry it with us wherever we go and in whatever we do.

This word beginning with 'F' prevents us from being the very best that we already are, every single day.

Welcome to failure.

So much more than a single word, it has become a phenomenon.

Now, let me ask you a question – it is the most power-ful question I was ever asked in my life.

Imagine if you simply could not fail:

What would you do?

Where would you go?

Who would you be?

Now. Hold that thought – put any other thought or question out of your mind.

Stop reading for a while – go away from your usual place of work or where you are right now, find a place on your own, and do what so few of us ever do: listen.

Listen to your surroundings – tune in to every sound – separate each and every one.

Listen to the silences in between – and allow the power of those silences to enter your mind.

As wonderful visions and thoughts and possibilities in all areas of your life flood in, welcome them.

Think about the word 'success' and what it means to you. And remember, your success is personal to you – it is private to you and it is yours to define. So for a few moments allow the word success to enter your mind.

What hopes, thoughts, visions and dreams does it bring with it?

Open the gates holding back your dreams, and let those dreams flow through your body, your spirit and your self, warming you into a lovely bright glow.

And as you glow, I want to share three ideas:

1 **You are a unique and amazing person – and you have in your head right now a capacity to create, evolve and achieve that is bigger than the biggest computer that has ever, and will ever, be built.**

2 **When you were born, you were born with only two fears:**
   - **A fear of falling over.**
   - **A fear of loud noises.**
   Every other fear that you have, you have learned, and you can unlearn them, any time you choose.

3 **You have within you awesome gifts, talents and abilities that, when awoken, will literally astound you.**

No matter what your age, your background or your present challenges, you have everything inside you, right now, to achieve anything you want.

Of course, many other people will tell you that you do not.

I spent the first thirty-four years of my life believing that I had 'something missing', something that I just couldn't find to make me whole. And one day, in a single breath, I understood why I had never found it.

Because there was nothing to 'find' that was 'missing'. I was spending all of my time searching for something that was nowhere to be found. I was looking 'without'.

And then, quite suddenly I found everything, by looking within.

My life has been completely different for the last eleven years, more fulfilling in each and every day. More hope, more joy, more love and peace. And I now live a very different life to the one I led before.

You may have had the same experience. Many people look back on their past and see it in different, distinct phases – childhood, school, a single life, marriage, parenthood, etc. Each of these can be seen as totally different lives – whole lifetimes in themselves.

And when we move forward in this way it can seem like we are being reborn into our new life.

And when we are born, or reborn, the word failure doesn't feature in our personal dictionary or understanding. And so it is not a 'natural' feeling at all, indeed, it is totally 'unnatural', and can be removed any time we choose.

Whether you remove failure from your life will depend a lot on the choices you make and may even be influenced by the country you live in, for different countries across the world have very different attitudes towards 'success'.

When business is bad in some countries, like Thailand, for example, where they do not recognize unhappiness, people pull together and say, 'Come on, we can pull through, we can sort this out if we work together.' By contrast, when the economy and business is going well in some countries, like the UK, the newspapers only have one headline:

`Don't worry, there's a recession just around the corner`

When I am asked to speak at conferences, if I am introduced as a 'motivational speaker' in some countries, it is the kiss of death. As the Chairman says, 'Here's David Taylor, he is going to inspire you,' almost everyone in the room folds their arms and looks away – as if saying to themselves (and each other), 'Watch out, everyone, here comes one of those loud-mouthed evangelist types. No thank you – I've had all the inspiration I can handle for today.'

The experience is quite different in America. I was in Los Angeles recently speaking with a group of about 100 people. I started off in my normal, low-key way of telling them that although we had never met: 'I just KNOW that I am in a room full of giants, who will never, ever experience failure again.'

The room erupted, people were standing and clapping. One chap was standing on his seat at the back of the room shouting, 'GO, BRIT, GO.'

During the first break there were lots of hugs.

Different countries, different people, different reactions.

But there is one story that is universally the same. And if you are wondering when I will get to the 'business' message, all will now be explained, in just one paragraph.

Over the last twenty years, we have spent billions of global currency – that's billions – on training, on consultancy, on change initiatives, yet the vast majority of organizations have at best stood completely still, and most people remain unfulfilled.

Why?

What have we done wrong?

What do we have to do to make sure this is not repeated, to make sure the future is very different from the past, in both our professional and personal lives?

That is the question I set out to answer in this book.

I am not a psychologist, I am not an academic, I am an ordinary guy who has spent twenty years working for organizations around the world, and who for the last five years has been seeking the answer to just one question.

Is it possible that success has structure?

Could success have a formula, that, when followed, brings us what we want? A simple, repeatable, powerful how-to-achieve formula?

And so I embarked on my 'research'. I worked with people from all walks of life – from people born into poverty, to golfers and footballers, to some of the most successful organizations and leaders in the world.

I read personal-development and self-help books (beyond the first chapter!).

I attended conferences and events throughout the world. I listened to tapes and CDs.

I became a 'success' junkie.

And then, one day, I made a realization. It had taken me three years (sorry, I am a bit slow).

I realized that every single book, every single speaker, every single tape, said exactly the same thing. There is a formula for guaranteed success. I will now share it with you. Before I do, remember three important things:

1 **This is not my formula, it is yours. It has been yours from the moment you were born – it is your birthright.**

2 **This formula belongs to no-one, it belongs to everyone.**

3 **Every single time you have achieved 'success', i.e. anything you want, in your life, you followed this formula.**

And here it is:

The formula for guaranteed success:

1 **Know where you want to go.**

2 **Know where you are now.**

3 **Know what you have to do, to get to where you want to go.**

4 **Do it!**

Silence.

Right now, you are in one of three groups:

A third of you will simply scream, 'YES, I'm with you all the way, David. Thank you for putting it so simply – now go for it with the rest of the book.'

A third of you will stop and think, 'Eh? I've never heard success put so simply, it's always been so full of jargon and mystery before, but I am prepared to read on, David, and see what you say next.'

And a third of you will be yelling at me, 'NO! Who is

this weirdo? Certainly not someone I want to know, let alone believe.'

In which of these three categories do you belong?

Please stick around to find out if you are correct . . .

You are completely right. Well done. Your answer is the correct one.

But how do I know which third you are in?

I don't. I can't look into your eyes, I can't see you, and I can't see your reactions.

However, I know that you are right, because whichever one you chose is the way you will live your life, from now on, and the way you will read this book.

After all, there is no right or wrong, there is only what takes you closer to your dream, and the life you were born to lead, and what takes you further away. And although the 'F' word will often kick in, we must remember that failure is a noun, and so the only fear it holds for us is in the meaning we give it. Here are three powerful ways to leave failure behind

○ **Take control of it by giving it one definition.** Failure is given so much power by having so many different definitions in our lives. And so we use it every day in many different situations. By giving it a single definition we take control of it. I define failure as giving up, and on the really important thing's in my life, I simply never give up. And so, I never fail.

○ **Remove it, by making it too confusing to understand.** Just as George Orwell brilliantly confused the definition of freedom in his book *1984*. And it is very confusing, as if there is one overriding thing that people who succeed all agree on, it's this – they would never have achieved what they did if they had not 'failed' along the way. So, in order to succeed we have to fail, therefore failure is an inherent part of success. Post-Its are a classic example – they were invented by mistake, as were the sweets, Liquorice Allsorts. So failure = success. Confused now? Good.

● **Let's learn from people who have achieved success.** Many people who achieve their dreams say that you have to 'fail' in order to succeed. 'Failure' is a critical component to success and a prerequisite to succeeding. Therefore it can't be 'failure' at all.

In reverse, success is also a noun, and so the only wonder it holds for us is in the meaning we give it. We take total control of success when we make it personal to us; it belongs to us, and is ours to define.

These form some of the seven principles of Naked Leadership, which run throughout this book:

1 **Success is a formula, and it is simple.**

2 **This formula does not 'belong' to anyone – it belongs to everyone.**

3 **To be successful, you need rely on no-one, other than yourself.**

4 **Success is whatever you want it to be, you define it.**

5 **Success can happen very fast, often in a heartbeat.**

6 **Everyone has value, can be anything they want, and is a leader.**

7   The biggest mystery of life is to discover who we truly are.
These seven principles can be summarized in just one sentence which outlines the aim of this book:

Many people will tell you to aim higher – be *more*, be the very best that you can be.

I invite you to be the very best that you already are.

This book will provide you with literally hundreds of real, specific and practical actions to take. Either take those that will help you get to where you want to go, and make them happen, or do the complete opposite.

It is your choice.

There are no general answers in life, there are only choices.

If there was only one way to be a wonderful parent, or a partner or leader, we would all know it, do it, and life would be, well, very boring.

And by making choices, we find not the answers, but *our answers*, those things that work, and those things that do not, *for us*.

Welcome to The Naked Leader, and to discovering the life you were born to lead: Welcome Home.

Your book, your choice. Please read this book in any order you wish. But if you wish to follow the chapters in the order they were written, please go to Chapter 6, on page 57.

Book One

Reclaim Your Birthright

Book One

why?

Children are always asking questions. They usually ask the most embarrassing questions at the most unexpected times.

'Mummy, what's sex?' just as you are about to drop them off at school.

'Daddy, why do you swear when you tell me not to?' in front of your best friends at dinner.

Of course, the time they really love to ask questions is just before they go to bed. Children understand delaying tactics better than anyone.

And most of their questions begin with the word 'Why?'

Next time you have a lot of energy have a go yourself.

I had a go once, with a friend's child, we'll call her Claire.

C: 'Why do you put the rubbish out the same day every week?'

D: 'Because that's the only day they collect it.'

C: 'Why?'

D: 'Because they collect from different areas on different days, and they collect from us on a Tuesday.'

C: 'Why?'

D: 'I don't know.'

C: 'Why?'

There was a long pause. I then went into a lengthy explanation on resource management and allocation, along with as much as I knew about landfill sites. It was probably not entirely accurate, but I was proud that it would have satisfied an exam board on rubbish collection.

By the time I had finished, 'Claire' had lost interest, I was exhausted, and I honestly wondered whether our children (and other people's) ask the question to get an answer, or just to wind us up.

And then I thought: Children ask many, many questions, and we are expected to answer.

And if we don't know all the answers, we make stuff up.

So what happens when adults ask the same questions, especially of ourselves? You know the sort of questions I mean, the big questions.

And the biggest question of all is: 'Why?'

It may be myth, it may be true, but the story goes that in the Seventies Oxford University held a philosophy exam, where the only question on the paper was: 'Why?' One student answered, 'Why not?' and was given full marks, 100 per cent. Another answered, 'Because,' and achieved 75 per cent.

Anyone who has ever taken an exam will wonder why

the examiners didn't add the word, 'Discuss', although apparently every other student wrote the customary thousands of words, probably because they felt it was expected of them.

And so, wherever you are right now, put the book down for a moment as you ask yourself the same question:

Why?

It's a massive question that has many meanings depending on who you are.

- **If you are clear about where you want to go, do you know *why* you want this future?**

- **Why do we do what we do at any one time? What decides our priorities, choices and actions?**

- **And the biggest question of all, who are you and why are you here?**

Looking back, recent centuries can be characterized by different themes:

The eighteenth century was very much about How? How do things work? The century of inventions, when we discovered and learned so much about how 'things' operate.

The nineteenth was the century of Where? Geographical discovery, new lands, maps and adventure.

The twentieth century built up to What? What do you do for a living? What religion are you? What do you earn?

And in my opinion the twenty-first century will be about one question:

Why . . .

● **Am I here?**

● **Do I do what I do?**

● **Do I want what I want?**

Massive questions will be asked this century, long after you and I have departed this earth.

And if we ask the right questions, we will get the right answers. Not THE answers of course, but OUR answers.

And to me Oxford University should have awarded top marks to the guy who wrote 'because'. Because, when we have a purpose, we are on purpose. When we discover why we are here, we feel it all over us.

And we start *knowing*.

You have no evidence, you just know. That you are as one with yourself, the world and everyone in it.

And the results are there, long before you have thought about methods and strategies. That is one trait of success-ful people, they know the why and the what long before they even begin to think about the how.

You just know that what you are doing is *right*, for you.

It is impossible to describe, and is very very personal:

> It is like a warm river of energy flowing through us;
> It is a tingle of excitement that runs through us every time we think about our dream, and what we will achieve;
> It makes us cry with joy at the discovery of something new or more likely something that has been within us for so long;
> It is an awesome feeling of personal power.

You may feel you never had such feelings before, but you did. You had them when you were born and, many people believe, while you were in your mother's womb.

And so, next time you have such a feeling – perhaps a sudden rush of well-being, a fantastic glow all over – stop, smile, and be a human being.

Priorities

One hundred years from now,
It will not matter
What kind of car I drove,
What kind of house I lived in,
How much I had in my bank account,
Nor what my clothes looked like.
But the world may be a little better because
I was important
In the life of a child.

If you wish to follow the chapters in the order they were written, please go to Chapter 16, on page 129.

destiny one

Think back to a time, to a moment when you had a fantastic idea, an amazing insight, or a new ambition. It may have been lying dormant inside you for a long time, or it may have come to you in a flash of inspiration.

It may have happened on a leadership course, in a team meeting, or while you were in the bath. It may have been for yourself, for your relationships, for your team or your organization.

Wherever, whenever and whatever it was, when it came to you, it made your body tingle, your head soar and your heart begin to dance.

What a fantastic feeling that is, waking up to your astounding, awesome abilities.

And the first thing you want to do is to share your idea – an idea shared is pleasure doubled, after all. And so you share it with someone close to you:

- **Your partner**

- **A work colleague**

- **A friend**

Their reaction is positive, supportive, and so you ask for their 'honest' opinion. The very asking of this, of course, invites what happens next . . .

You always know when the Dreaded Three-letter Words (DTWs) are coming. It's like your partner, colleague or friend has telegraphed them ahead – it's like they have just left their home base and they are coming your way. And they are coming your way with the added power of being delivered through your trusted confidante . . .

They start to give you their 'honest' opinion by asking you if you are sure you really want to hear what they have to say. You say yes, and your body tightens. After all, they would hardly ask you if you wanted to hear what they had to say if they were going to say: 'That's the most FANTASTIC idea I have ever heard, you are a genius, the champagne's on me.'

Their preparation in asking is needed, of course:

- **To give the DTWs time to travel into their head.**

- **To prepare you for the worst.**

It's a bit like preparing someone for bad news.

When I was younger, if one of our dogs died (we had lots of dogs over lots of years) my dad would always drive

THE NAKED LEADER EXPERIENCE

my brother Alan and me into a cul-de-sac and park the car at the end. He would turn to us and say, 'I am afraid I have some very bad news for you.'

It was very caring of him. Of course, the trouble is that by the time I reached the age of twelve, every time we went anywhere near a cul-de-sac my whole body shook with dread.

Anyway, you have said you want to hear your trusted friend or colleague's thoughts, and they always seem to start so positively:

'I can see why you want to become a pilot . . .'

'I think it is great that you have this ambition . . .'

'I really do support you in what you are saying . . .'

And now it's fill-in-the-blank time – what word do they always say next?

Yes, it's the first of the two DTWs. Here it comes . . .

'BUT . . .'

Which sounds in your head, your heart and your very soul, like:

'BUUUUUUUUUUUUUUUUUUUUUUUUUUUUUUUT.'

And then, just as you are knocked back, just as you are beginning to think it wasn't such a very good idea, after all, just when you are about to dream a smaller dream, they do a double whammy on you. They bring in the second DTW straight away.

It's like being in a boxing match against Muhammad Ali – he's got you on the ropes, and then he delivers the old one-two.

One: 'But . . .'

Two: 'HOW . . . ?'

'HOOOOOOOOOOOOOOOOOOOOOOOOOOOOOW?'

And most people's dreams end right there. Because while BUT is a negative and it puts you on the defensive, at least it's not you that's saying it.

But (sic) HOW is the real killer, because it's a question. It's the question to end millions of dreams, so much potential and so many ambitions.

And why is that? Because you don't know HOW, yet.

BUT if you say that . . .

'I don't know.'

They will give you a look that says – or worse still, they will actually say – 'Well, if you don't know how, isn't that a clue in itself? If you don't know how, is this really the right dream for you? If you don't know how, then who does?'

Please remember the next sentence for the rest of your life – remember it with hope, with belief and with the power to know that in a contest between this sentence and BUT and HOW combined, this sentence wins every time:

IT DOESN'T MATTER – YOU DON'T NEED TO KNOW THE HOW, YOU ONLY NEED TO KNOW THE *WHAT* RIGHT NOW.

People who achieve success know the *what* before, sometimes long before, they know the *how*.

The *what* is their dream, it is their vision, their aim, their life's purpose. And it is personal to them. Even if they are going to put it into powerful practice with their partner, their team, their organization, for now it is theirs.

So welcome the feeling of warmth that comes with an outstanding idea, insight or innovation – and as it arrives, pound it into your heart, your soul and your self. See yourself achieving your dream, right now.

Hear it, feel it, *experience* it.

Close your eyes and rejoice in it, right now. Because every single person who has ever dreamt of achieving anything in their lives sees it and hears it first.

As a commentator on the BBC said, 'To be a

Wimbledon champion, first you have to feel like a Wimbledon champion.'

And as Martin Luther King said, 'I have a dream.' (He did not say, 'I have a project plan and spreadsheet.')

Sir Terry Matthews, an entrepreneur, told me many years ago about his dream: 'I will bring golf's Ryder Cup to Wales.' And immediately everyone asked him, 'How?'

And Terry smiled a knowing, private and certain smile.

That was twenty odd years ago – and guess what? The Celtic Manor in Wales, built and owned by Terry, will be the home of the Ryder Cup. One dream comes true.

Terry did not know how, when he dreamt the *what* – if he had (build hotel and three golf courses, one being amongst the world's best), golf's biggest team championship would probably have stayed just a dream.

And finally, back to that conversation with your friend. It is not their fault that they are killing your dream, they are (probably) not doing it deliberately – although the more people you share it with, the sooner you will come up against someone who will do it maliciously.

However, there is one grain of hope in this discussion, and it is a total irony – if that person does not see how you can achieve your ambition, they will genuinely let you down gently, and manage your expectations, by saying BUT and HOW – after all, they do not want you to get hurt.

The irony is this – if they really, that's REALLY, don't think you can achieve your ambitions, your hopes and dreams are in for a boost. Whenever anyone TELLS us, over and over, that we cannot achieve something, or reach new heights, it has the reverse effect, because our mind automatically focuses on any idea that is put forward, however that idea is expressed. When we are told not to think about something, we think about it more!

Think about it. Did anyone ever tell you that you would NEVER achieve something – and part of you, deep down, said, 'I'll show them . . .'?

Millions of people have had that experience. You can too, any time you choose. Just remember, you choose your own decisions, dreams and destiny.

The Contented Fisherman

The rich industrialist from the north was horrified to find the southern fisherman lying lazily beside his boat, smoking a pipe.

'Why aren't you fishing?' said the industrialist.

'Because I have caught enough fish for the day,' said the fisherman.

'Why don't you catch some more?'

'What would I do with it?'

'You could earn more money,' was the reply. 'And with that extra money you could have a motor fixed to your boat and go into deeper waters and catch more fish. Then you would make enough to buy nylon nets. These would bring you more fish and more money. Soon you would have enough money to own two boats . . . maybe even a fleet of boats. Then you would be a rich man like me.'

'What would I do then?' replied the fisherman.

'Then,' said the industrialist, 'then, you could really enjoy life.'

To which the fisherman replied: 'What do you think I am doing right now?'

Anthony De Mello

THE NAKED LEADER EXPERIENCE

If you wish to follow the chapters in the order they were written, please go to Chapter 42, on page 355.

long live dreams

It does not matter how old you are, your background or your present position, you can still lead the life you were born to lead. All you have to do is choose.

We have preconceptions about age that may not help us – children have to learn, 'life begins at forty' and 'you can't teach an old dog new tricks'.

It all comes down to dreams, success and decisions. And different generations can help each other more than they realize.

It starts with the moment we are born, naked, and full of amazing potential and possibilities. Our first five years are critical, we take in so much. And then we have school, which has such an impact on our beliefs:

Hands up, those of you who learnt at school that you were not very good at mathematics? Were you right?

Now, put your hand up if you learnt at school that you were outstanding at the sciences – physics, chemistry and the like. Were you right?

Of course you were, we always are.

When we are young, we are so curious, energetic, and hungry for life. And then we grow up. When, exactly? Legally, we know when we are grown up – a certain age for cinema films, for driving and for marriage. But when do we, the real *we*, grow up? Is it when we lose our curiosity, our questioning and our dreams? The very skills we need to be all that we already are.

Perhaps, whatever age we are, it will help us to remember, recapture and relive some of our childhood.

For when we lose our dreams and desires, we lose a part of our selves. And when we do that, it has a major impact on our self-esteem, on our enjoyment in life, on us and everyone around us.

Our dreams, hopes and ambitions can be reclaimed – at any age, and at any time we choose. And when we do that for our selves, we send out massive signals of hope to our next generation. Sadly, when we are unsure about our selves we send out conflicting messages.

Picture the confusion in their minds: your child comes rushing into the house, full of life, leaping around with joy, and we tell them to 'calm down'. Later, they are quiet and upset, so we say simply 'cheer up'.

And the other things we say to young people:

'Grow up.'

'Stop behaving like a child.'

'When I was your age . . .'

Often we say these things because we have lost touch with our selves. If we as adults are not at one with our selves, we will never connect with others, and to be as one ourselves, we need to reconnect with childhood things: emotions, honesty, dreams.

Often, we make assumptions about young people's intelligence.

Hamish Taylor, CEO of Vision Consulting UK, shared a lovely story about how we often underestimate the knowledge of our children. Listening to Van Morrison, Hamish's five-year-old son Donald asked what instrument was being played. It was a harmonica, but how to describe that in language a five-year-old would understand?

Hamish used as simple terms as he could muster and the conversation proceeded:

> *Hamish: 'It's like a mouth organ, where music is produced by either sucking or blowing and by moving the instrument left and right.'*
>
> *Donald: 'Thank you, Dad.'*
>
> *Hamish: 'That's OK – why did you ask?'*
>
> *Donald: 'Oh no reason really, it just sounded a bit like a harmonica.'*

Children know far more than we often give them credit for. And children know how to dream. Why should they have all the fun? Why shouldn't adults have dreams, great big stonking ones?

In the film *Big*, Tom Hanks plays David, a man who wishes he was a boy again, and he gets his wish – in spirit and mind, not in body. It is hilarious, and it is painful, as it shows us what we can lose, and what we can remember, and regain, as we grow older.

There is one scene in which he is part of a team being presented with an idea for a new toy. Clearly this is an important meeting for the presenter, and the rest of the meeting quickly agree with what is being proposed – a robot that turns into a building.

David plays with the toy throughout the presentation (how rude) and, at the end, politely puts up his hand to speak (do this at your next project meeting and see the reactions). He says: 'I don't get it.'

Faced with all of the market research and politics in the room (which he doesn't notice), he speaks his gut feelings with childlike innocence: 'It's a robot who turns into a building – what's so great about that?'

Enjoy awakening the child within. I am not suggesting that you cause mayhem in project meetings when a new initiative is presented, by raising your hand and saying you just don't 'get it'.

I am not suggesting you play with a train set, or imagine you are driving the next train you are on.

Unless you want to . . .

Unless you choose to . . .

I am suggesting that sometimes, when we feel down, when life doesn't seem to be going our way, when we want a better life, all we have to do is:

Remember to rekindle our dreams.

Remember to rejoice in our growing up.

And remember, and reclaim, our birthright to be anything, and anyone, we choose to be.

If, like me, you grew up in the Sixties and Seventies, enjoy these memories . . .

If you grew up in the Eighties and after, simply imagine . . .

As children, we would ride in cars with no seat belts or air bags. Our baby cots were covered with bright-coloured

THE NAKED LEADER EXPERIENCE

lead-based paint. We had no childproof lids on medicine bottles, doors or cabinets, and when we rode our bikes, we had no helmets. (Not to mention hitchhiking to town as a young kid!)

We would spend hours building go-carts out of scraps and then ride down the hill, only to find out we forgot the brakes. After running into the bushes a few times we learnt to solve the problem.

We would leave home in the morning and play all day, as long as we were back when the streetlights came on. No-one was able to reach us all day. No mobile phones. Unthinkable.

We played dodgeball and sometimes the ball would really hurt. We got cut and broke bones and broke teeth and there were no lawsuits from these accidents. They were accidents. No-one was to blame but us. Remember accidents? We had fights and punched each other and got black and blue and learnt to get over it.

We ate cakes, bread and butter, and drank sugary pop but we were never overweight . . . we had pleasure from our food rather than worrying about what we were eating. We shared one bottle of pop with four friends, from one bottle and no-one died from this?

We did not have PlayStations, Nintendo 64, XBoxes, video games, all 99 channels on Sky Digital TV, video tape movies, surround sound, mobile phones, personal computers, Internet chat rooms . . . we had friends. We went outside and found them.

Our actions were our own. Consequences were expected. There was no-one to hide behind. The idea of a parent bailing us out if we broke a law was unheard of. They actually sided with the law, imagine that!

This generation has produced some of the best

risk-takers and problem solvers and inventors, ever. The past fifty years has seen an explosion of innovation and new ideas.

With thanks to Brinley Platts.

If you wish to follow the chapters in the order they were written, please go to Chapter 35, on page 299.

talkback

You may not always be able to control the events that happen to you or around you. However, you can always control what meaning you give to these events, and how you react to them.

Do you enjoy flying? If so, think of a friend who hates it. Or if you can't stand flying, bring someone who loves it into your mind.

Let's assume you love it. There you are, relaxing just before you take off. You glance at your watch to see whether you will be arriving on time. All is well with the world.

A few rows behind you, you notice your friend squirming awkwardly, nervously eyeing the wings to see if they are thicker than balsa wood and wondering how such thin bits of metal can possibly be strong enough to carry the weight of the plane, its passengers and their luggage. And they are sweating (if it is a man) or perspiring (if it is a woman).

That's why you are not sitting next to your friend, by the way!

Now, what's the difference here? Why are you cool, calm and collected and your friend is a soggy mess?

Well, it's not the plane.

And it's not the seats.

In fact, it's only one thing.

It's your **attitude**, compared with that of your friend. Your attitude is the meaning you give to any event, or anything, in your life.

Different people, different attitudes.

Now one for the men (women will find it hilarious though): you leave work and you decide to buy some beautiful flowers for your girlfriend/partner/wife (delete as appropriate). By coincidence your friend is at the shop, on the same mission – also to buy flowers for your partner. No, just kidding. They are there to buy flowers for their respective loved one. There are just two identical bouquets left in the shop. You choose yours, because they are beautiful, with such radiant, complementary colours – and because they are cheap, but look expensive. You both walk out of the shop, say goodbye to each other, and then separately walk out with two identical bunches of flowers, and straight into two completely different realities.

Your friend goes home, presents the flowers to his girlfriend, wife, etc., who immediately throws her arms around him and says, 'Thank you, my darling. They are absolutely beautiful, I love you so much.' And with that she gives your friend loving and suggestive looks that leave him in no doubt that the flowers have done the trick.

Meanwhile, you go home, and present the flowers to your partner, who immediately throws them to one side, slaps you in the face and says, 'What have you been up to then?'

Now, what's different here?

Well, it's not the flowers.

And it's not the amount you spent.

In fact, it's only one thing.

It's your partner's **attitude**, compared with that of your friend's partner.

In other words, the meaning she gave to what you did compared to the meaning your friend's partner gave. And so it is with life, in all that we do.

Right now, the words I am writing will mean different things to different readers because, quite literally, we are all living in our own realities. How we communicate with ourselves (our private Talkback) determines the meaning we give to everything, which determines how we react to thoughts, feelings and events. And this is our **attitude**.

The first sign of madness, is talking to ourselves.

The second sign of madness, is arguing with ourselves.

And the final sign of madness, is losing the argument.

And yet we do this, all the time. So, why does this happen?

Because of the way we work as human beings, because of the way we talk to each other, and because of the way we talk back to ourselves.

We all experience events and circumstances differently because we all live in a unique world of our own making. This derives from the way our brains filter information.

Generalization, deletion and distortion are three major filtering processes by which we make sense of the information our senses are picking up – and, of course, by which we misunderstand everyone else's point of view. Think about how easy it is to make broad generalizations about people and situations based on minimal evidence!

Well of course, people always say it's easy to spot generalizations. You just have to listen.

Have you ever sold your house? If you have, you will probably have noticed that as soon as you made the decision to do so, 'For Sale' boards appeared outside dozens of houses in your area!

*Now, of course, this is not really true. What happened was that you now **noticed** that other houses were up for sale, whereas before you made the decision to sell, you had not noticed! This is a perfectly normal and automatic process of **deletion**, where information you don't need is deleted from your conscious awareness. In this way we are left with only data that we need to function in our current contexts – it's a process the brain uses to be efficient.*

No matter how often we see something, we rarely see it all! We delete the information that's not needed from our conscious thought.

*Another filter, **distortion**, works both for us and against us.*

Distortion forms the basis of innovation, creativity and evolutionary thought. It is how we alter our perceptions and thereby change the experience we receive from our senses. By using this process we can create and enjoy art, music, literature – we can access the world of our imagination. But we also give ourselves, and others, a really hard time with distortions!

We mind-read:

   'You are angry with me.'
   'How do you know?'

THE NAKED LEADER EXPERIENCE

We make value judgements:

  'It's bad to do that.'

  'According to who?'

We interpret:

  'He doesn't like me, he hasn't called.'

  'How does him not calling mean he doesn't like you?'

So, every waking moment of every day, we are responding to our own version of reality, created by the filters we have put on events.

We quickly evaluate this by attaching meaning to the event – is it good/bad, pleasurable/unpleasurable, positive/negative . . .

This produces a set of emotions – happiness, anxiety, comfort, fear, excitement, stress . . .

These, in turn, determine what action we take, how we respond: what we do.

Which determines what happens: our results.

And so the loop continues . . . in increasing cycles of helpful or unhelpful stimuli and responses. Effectively, what we do in creating our own response is to create our own reality.

Our habitually limited thinking rarely encourages the wider perspective. But very often a slight change of perspective is all it takes to make a significant change of meaning. People who move forward do so because they choose helpful meanings for the circumstances they find themselves in.

Paul Crittenden
www.peakorganisation.com

Beware these phrases:

- **'There are two sides to an argument'**
  (There are many sides)

- **'You're on a different planet'**
  (Absolutely, and so are you!)

- **'Get real'**
  (And whose reality would you like me to get?)

When we understand how our brains work, without all of the psychobabble, it puts us in a very powerful position. We understand other people's points of view, see events in a different light, and, above all, we choose our own actions and reactions, our attitude.

Indeed, the one thing you have absolute control over is your attitude. And when you take control of it, you take control of your life.

When two people get locked in their own Talkback, it leads to disagreement, argument or worse.

The most powerful way to overcome this, and to understand each other, is through a mutual understanding session. This method has been used to resolve some of the biggest disputes around the world.

Two groups, One and Two, take totally opposite views.

Group One states their 'case' – their beliefs, what they feel, why they feel it and what they want to see happen about it.

Group Two puts aside their own thoughts and beliefs and, instead, they repeat back to Group One what Group One have just said, but (and here's the powerful twist)

THE NAKED LEADER EXPERIENCE

they do so as if they are Group One. They speak the words exactly as if they were the people believing them.

Then you break.

Then you do the same in reverse.

Group Two states their 'case' – their beliefs, what they feel, why they feel it and what they want to see happen about it.

Group One then repeats back to Group Two what Group Two have just said, but (and here's the powerful twist) they do so as if they are Group Two. They speak the words exactly as if they were the people believing them.

If you wish to follow the chapters in the order they were written, please go to Chapter 23, on page 195.

crossing the rubicon

Crossing the Rubicon is a phrase that means there is no going back. It represents an emotional breakthrough, choosing to make a true decision, and only going forward.

On my travels, was I destined to become a parrot of the bleedin' obvious?

Or was there any element of this formula that cuts through and across every leadership and success book I had ever read, about which people disagreed? I am not talking about people who disagree with the formula itself – I am talking about people who disagree with the navigation.

I found two areas, one minor, one major.

The minor one relates to whether people include 'Know where you are now'. Many people I spoke to said,

'Know where you want to go, know what you have to do, and do it.'

I feel it is very important to include knowing where we are now because it enables us to:

- **Take ownership of our lives – one of the most personal and powerful things we can ever do.**

- **Open up our minds and hearts to realize the extra-ordinary potential inside each and every one of us.**

- **Encourage people to take action now, before they end up having huge regrets and carrying excess and unwanted baggage on their shoulders for the rest of their lives.**

And now the major one:

Many people, 'gurus' and companies I met argued that while the formula is right, my emphasis in presentations was wrong.

I was always emphasizing the third stage – 'Know what you have to do . . .'

They said to me, 'Surely it's not the knowing what you have to do that matters, it's the doing it – the action.'

As Nike would say, 'Just Do It.'

OK, put on a pair of Nike shoes and run east looking for the perfect sunset. You won't find it, no matter how fast you run.

And now, think about your organization, and please be absolutely honest here, ask yourself:

Do you ever have a meeting in your organization, say a weekly project meeting on a Monday, where you make a decision, and then you all get together the following week and you find you are still discussing the same decision?

Of course you do. I have never met an organization that works in any other way.

And so we do nothing. Or, more likely, we seem to do everything we can to delay making a decision. More information needed, more time to consider, more experts to be consulted.

Have you seen how long Royal and other Commissions take to investigate something? Years.

So, back to your workplace – even if you know where you want this project to go and you probably know what you have to do to move it closer to its conclusion, you will delay making a true decision. Making a decision and then changing your mind a week later is the same as not making any decision at all. Similarly, a decision not carried through is not a decision at all.

The word decision is based on the Latin 'cision' – literally to cut off all other options.

Not very comfortable. But ask yourself, are you really comfortable, being comfortable?

And so we argue it's not very practical.

Another example – New Year's resolutions.

What was yours this year? How long did it last?

It is in the true decisions you make, that your destiny is shaped. And it's not the length of time it may take to make such a decision; it's when you choose to make one.

So, what is the best way to make a true decision?

To make one! Set a time limit, or a key moment from which you will not return, and make one. Make it with every ounce of belief, energy and strength you have. Do this, and you are halfway there.

When you make a true decision in a project, in your team or at work, go round the room and check that it is a true decision. Watch the looks on people's faces – an uneasy balance between discomfort at making a real decision that you won't go back on, and excitement at making a real decision that you won't go back on!

There are three additional reasons that true decisions are so powerful, aside from setting you on a clear and certain course of action:

⬤ **They are so rare.**

They set you apart from such a large percentage of the population – or your company from your competitors.

⬤ **They seem to set in course an unstoppable chain of events . . .**

When we know where we are going, with no Dream B, life stands by to help us achieve it. I am talking about Synchronicity, how when you commit your mind, body and spirit to a certain outcome, life will provide the resources you need.

How?

Because when you are set on achieving something, you are more open minded, you spot the resources, help and people you will need to see you through, because you are focused and looking out for them.

⬤ **Self-fulfilling prophecies.**

We've all experienced these – how events seem to support our belief systems, how every day can be an adventure, or not . . .

You ask your son (or husband!) to go and fetch the salt. He says, 'I don't know where it is.' You shout through to

THE NAKED LEADER EXPERIENCE

the kitchen (assuming he has managed to find the kitchen!), 'It's in the middle cupboard.'

You hear his huffing and puffing – fetching the salt has been his biggest challenge today – and I am not being facetious! He opens up the middle cupboard and you know what is coming next.

'It's not here.' He loves shouting that because it proves he is right, he did not know where it was.

'Yes it is.'

'No it's not.'

(This goes on while blood pressures rise.)

And then you get up. Storm into the kitchen, walk up to the cupboard and, right in front of his very eyes, pick up the salt.

You then turn round and gobsmack him completely by saying: 'Don't worry; I know you couldn't see it, because for you it wasn't there.'

Because he did not see it. Quite literally, he had convinced himself it was not there – he had told himself it was not there. So to him, well, to be more accurate, to his subconscious, it was invisible. Until you touched it – then it came rushing back into his view.

What has this to do with anything?

Everything! Because when we believe something to be true, we see the world in that way.

Take the writing of this book – I have shared many stories, my own and those of others, and quotes and anecdotes, to support my fundamental message: for you to be the very best that you already are.

Question: could I have used different quotes and stories and references to show the opposite, to show that you are not really capable of achieving very much in life, and that leadership and success are for other people and not for you?

Of course I could. I would simply use different stories, sources and quotes.

But, in truth, I would find it difficult to put forward such a negative message, because I am so focused on success I don't have a lot of time for giving up.

And this applies to everyone.

When we set a dream, decide we will achieve it, and we take the first step, life is on our side. Because we believe, we know so deeply that we will achieve this, that we will find every single piece of help we need along the way.

Self-fulfilling prophecies work for us, or against us. Either way, they will prove us right.

When I was seventeen, I was having a driving lesson with my mum and older brother, Alan. It is not the happiest memory of my life, and I'm sure it was no picnic for them, either.

I was driving along, when suddenly my mum shouted, 'You're going to hit that kerb.'

Alan joined in: 'Yes, you are.'

At the time I don't recall being anywhere near the kerb, but that was about to change, big time.

My mum was getting hysterical now – after all, we were doing five miles per hour.

'You're going to hit that kerb,' she said over and over.

And of course, I did.

And she said, 'I knew you were going to hit that kerb.'

She and I have laughed about this many times since and thank goodness she said kerb and not lamppost!

If you've got an old carpet, this one is fun:

Have someone carry a very full drink through from the kitchen – or, better still, more than one glass on a

THE NAKED LEADER EXPERIENCE

tray – and say over and over, 'You're going to spill it.'

Or even, 'Don't spill it.'

It has the same effect (putting the idea of spilling into their mind). And watch what happens.

I jest, of course. You will be saying, 'You are brilliant at carrying drinks,' etc.

So it is in our companies, in all that we do.

And so we move from knowing what we have to do, and deciding to do it, to taking action, and there are only three things we need to know here:

1 There is no right or wrong action.

There is only what takes you closer to where you want to be, and what takes you further away. If what you do takes you closer, do more of the same.

If it takes you further away, do something different, or give up – your choice – and as you come back with more action and a relentless persistence, you are discovering the

2 HOOOOOOOOOOOOOOOOOOOOOOOOOOOOOW?

To achieve your dream. You may remember this was a nasty word when we did not know the answer. Now we are finding out in the most powerful way, by actually taking positive steps forward.

When we close off all other options, it means we will accept no alternative outcome than the one we have decided to go for.

This does not mean we do not have different plans, ways to achieve the one outcome.

3 Celebrate rejection.

The word 'No' has long been one to avoid. Think about how often we hear it – job applications, rejection by potential lovers – all building on the number of times we heard it when we were children.

And so to perhaps the most important single paragraph in this entire book, if you, your team or your company wants to be successful.

Your success will depend on your persistence and belief, and this will be demonstrated by how much you celebrate any and all rejection that happens to you on your way to achieving your dream.

And the ultimate irony of success is that when you achieve what you know you will, it will be those people who told you that you couldn't do it who will be the first to say well done. And they will say they always knew you would do it.

We must take risks on our adventures, as leaders, teams and as organizations. When people make choices, they know this, and do it. As with everything in this book, please share this as widely as you wish.

Risk
To laugh is to risk appearing the fool
To weep is to risk appearing sentimental
To reach out to others is to risk involvement
To expose feelings is to risk exposing your true self
To place your ideas, your dreams before a crowd is to risk their loss.

THE NAKED LEADER EXPERIENCE

To love is to risk not being loved in return
To live is to risk dying
To hope is to risk despair
To try is to risk failure
But risks must be taken,
Because the greatest risk in life is to do nothing.

The person who risks nothing
Does nothing, has nothing, and is nothing.

They may avoid suffering and sorrow,
But they cannot learn, feel, change, grow, love, live.

Chained by their attitudes, they are a slave,
They forfeited their freedom.

Only the person who risks can be truly free

Author unknown

If you wish to follow the chapters in the order they were written, please go to Chapter 17, on page 135.

in a heartbeat!

Even after we have made a decision

- **To stop smoking**

- **To cure a phobia**

- **To gain more confidence**

why does personal change have to take so long?
There are four main reasons we feel change must take ages:

- **Conditioning**

We expect change to take ages, so it does – to learn a

language, to get the experience needed to do a job properly, or to break a habit. We are conditioned to believe we are on an uphill climb that's going to take for ever.

Experts tell us

Those that know, counsellors in particular, tell us change takes time, and often we have to discuss our deep-rooted problems in order to confront them and move forward.

And after many years, these theories are being disproved – and thank goodness for it. I've been there, discussing a problem from my past for forty-five minutes – reliving the horrors of every moment, and then having a counsellor say, 'Well, I think that was a good session.'

Please don't get me wrong, for certain deep-rooted illnesses counselling skills are of course needed. However, things can happen faster. Positive steps in the right direction can be taken immediately.

If you were listening to a scratched record or CD, would you play it again and again, or change the music?

We've never understood *how* to change fast

We've been bogged down in jargon. Simple how-to language that everyone can understand and master hasn't been available to us.

Cultures

Too often, we're led to believe that success takes years of hard work. And then we get our rewards by . . . dying.

Change doesn't need to be a long, drawn-out process. It

can happen very fast – in a heartbeat, in fact. It happens the moment we make a true decision, the moment we decide to act upon our dreams and ambitions, and stop allowing our doubts to overtake us.

We overestimate what we can achieve in a year, and underestimate what we can achieve in a moment.

Let's look at the *evidence* for that.

Remember, on the day you were born, you were only born with two fears: a fear of falling (which serves you well, as without this you would never learn to walk) and a fear of loud noises (which has largely disappeared by the time you reach your teenage years!).

Every other fear we have today, we have learned ourselves, and can be unlearned.

And to make the actual change faster, we have to make sure that the conditions that enable such a fast change are in place.

Think about the big changes in your life, when you reached a point beyond *should*, and arrived at *must*.

One crucial factor regarding change is whether you feel you are in control of those very circumstances, or do they happen at random?

Do you believe that:

Your life comes down to chance?

or

Your life comes down to choice?

If you decide the second, then change can happen in a heartbeat – you just need to make that heartbeat deliberate.

These are the most powerful ways to make change in your life happen, very fast. And there is only one single proviso, one rule, one 'given' – you must *want* to change.

Neuro Linguistic Programming – NLP (Richard Bandler and John Grindler)

1 The fastest way to make any change in your life

As-If

The fastest way to make any change in your life is to act 'as-if' that change has already been made.

(This information is detailed in book one – and is available to download free at *www.nakedleader.com/as-if*)

2 The fastest way to change how you feel:

If you have ever done anything in your life once, you are capable of doing it again, any time that you choose. This is clear to us when we hear a piece of music that meant something when we were younger – it may have been a first date or another special occasion. From that moment on, until our last moments on earth, wherever and whenever we hear that same piece of music, we automatically feel the same as we did when we first heard it.

This is called Association.

Now, we can take control of that feeling.

Whenever we feel unstoppable, amazing, fantastic, we simply choose a discrete and deliberate movement, such as touching our thumb and first finger. Any time you perform this action again, you will immediately recreate the same state.

It works just as well with events – if you are running well, playing chess well or simply enjoying what you are doing, make the movement.

The result: performance on demand.

3 **The fastest way to ensure any change you make sticks**

Neuro Associative Conditioning (Anthony Robbins).

Associate massive – that is MASSIVE – pain to the behaviours you do not want, and massive – that is MASSIVE – pleasure to the behaviours you desire.

In The Naked Leader *I had a dig at the founders of Neuro Linguistic Programming (NLP), Richard Bandler and John Grindler, who have recently been involved in litigation over who owns what. My comments attracted the wrath of many people and I invited one of these, Karen Marshall, an NLP Executive Leadership Coach whom I greatly respect, to a short debate with me. You choose the outcome.*

In the Red Corner, Karen Marshall

Although NLP has developed its own jargon, most NLP practitioners now use plain English. NLP has brought powerful techniques on rapport, learning the skills of great leaders, and choice, to the mass market. Its techniques are well proven, and the founders' falling-out is irrelevant to this. I have the highest respect for the genius of the originators of NLP. Their work and dedication to helping others achieve their desired outcomes is second to none.

David uses a lot of NLP, and the choices he writes about are at the very heart of NLP thinking, so he should be more supportive of something that is serving him so well!

In the Blue Corner, David Taylor

NLP is very powerful; no-one is denying that, it brings together many proven methods for powerful change. Sadly it has become too full of its own invented jargon, e.g. 'anchoring' and 'modelling', and obsessed with its own importance. This places the focus on the process itself and the power with the NLP practitioner, rather than on the results, and the person being helped. This is the wrong way round. And considering rapport is at its heart, Richard Bandler, especially, does his own discipline no favours by resorting to making lawyers richer, for which the reputation of NLP is poorer.

Please visit Karen on *www.optimafutura.com*.

The Little Bird

'Excuse me,' said a bird. 'You are older than I, so can you tell me where to find this thing they call the sky?'

'The sky,' said the older bird, 'is the thing you are in now.'

'Oh, this? But this is air. What I'm seeking is the sky,' said the disappointed bird as he flew away to search elsewhere.

If you wish to follow the chapters in the order they were written, please go to Chapter 19, on page 149.

the heart-stopping question

'There are two ways you can die. You can stop breathing or you can stop dreaming.'

Rocco Casciato

It stopped me in my tracks completely.

It was the most powerful and uncomfortable question I had ever been asked.

'How long are you going to be dead?'

The silence that followed seemed to last a lifetime.

I wanted to talk about faith. I wanted to ask what he meant. I wanted to curl up and think.

The question was asked of me by a very close friend of mine with a life-threatening illness, who will no longer be with us when you read this book.

He broke the silence first: 'In the film *Beetle Juice*, two of the leading characters die at the very beginning.' (Throws my chapter on Hollywood story structure, I thought, but didn't say.) 'One of them mentions they have a worry about something; the other person replies, *We're dead, I don't think we have very much to worry about any more.*'

I asked him where this was going, and he replied: 'There comes a moment when we decide to be all that we can be. When we appreciate all that we have and all that we are, and all that we can be.'

And he showed me this extract from a moving piece written by Peter Hughes, called 'A Love of Life', published here with the kind permission of Peter's wife Christine. Peter died from motor neurone disease, a wasting disease of the nerves and muscles, in Woking Hospice.

During the last few months many people have come up to me and said you do look well or, how do you keep so happy or, I am amazed at how you managed to cope.

These comments got me thinking how, until something like this happens, most people take life for granted . . .

. . . I believe I value life now more than when I was fully fit . . . it is a pity it takes something like ill-health to help us appreciate the joys of life. So it would be nice to think that even just one person reading this might stop, think, and look around and realize what they are missing by never having the time to stand and stare. Remember there are plenty of things to see in this world, and slowing down helps you appreciate them and have a love of life.

And he added:

THE NAKED LEADER EXPERIENCE

Love like you've never been hurt.

And dance like no-one is watching.

They say it takes a minute to find a special person, an hour to appreciate them, a day to love them, but then an entire life to forget them.

There is a very powerful exercise that Tony Robbins and other leadership presenters do with audiences. It is life changing in itself.

Known as 'the Dickens Experience' after Scrooge's visits through time in *A Christmas Carol*, the audience is relaxed, and then travels in their minds to the very point of their death, to their leaving this earth.

The facilitator skilfully leads them to imagine their lives, as if they have not achieved what they set out to, a life full of regrets and underachievement. And remember how powerful our imaginations are.

It is a devastating experience, must only be carried out by very experienced workshop leaders, and the results are astounding, as people 'remember' what they have not achieved and prepare to die full of remorse and regret.

And then they experience total relief as they are brought 'back' to the present day, and 'wake up' as if they are Ebenezer Scrooge himself waking on Christmas Day.

If there is ever an experience that makes people choose to change something in their lives, this is it.

And now I invite you to make some true decisions – decisions about things in your life that you know, deep down, need to be changed. And as you do so, close off each and every other alternative.

No more sitting on the fence!

> On gravestones, there is always a little dash between the dates that people lived. The first date is the year we were born, the second is the year we died, and the dash is our life.
>
> How's your 'dash' going?

Thanks to Paul and Karen Davies for sharing this brave and remarkable story. From Paul:

The experience of losing a child, although incredibly hard at the time, certainly provides a sort of marker, a bench-mark of where you have been, emotionally as well as physically, that you can draw upon in such a positive way. Many people often express how they cannot understand or believe how well we coped with everything . . . but you do. It brings out certain thoughts and behaviours that I think are always there. Just as in work, we learn from our experiences to become better at our job. I apply this to everything I do now and honestly believe I am a better person for it! For example, I never miss a school sports day now. Two hours of watching your children having lots of fun whilst you sit uncomfortably on a miniature chair in the middle of a field . . . but that two hours is precious to them, and for me I often think of all the extra hours I spent at work when Bethany was alive and adding them up and thinking, 'That's another day I could have spent with her.' I aim to see my family every day now, at least either the morning or evening, allowing ourselves the time to enjoy the views and activities of each other and sharing with them my thoughts. It puts a lot into perspective sometimes! By believing in yourself and your abilities to achieve, knowing what you have to draw upon is a very positive feeling. I also find that being open, and sharing these experiences with friends and colleagues can be very fulfilling. The balance of life becomes so much more real and meaningful. It's not always easy, but always more rewarding . . .

If you wish to follow the chapters in the order they were written, please go to Chapter 38, on page 319.

brand you

Personal branding has become a hot topic in recent years. You know the sort of thing. When you think of Tiger Woods, you think of a superbly talented sportsman who is capable of beating all opposition – a veritable mean machine of efficiency! Or Bill Gates – the massively successful businessman who has quite literally changed the way we live our lives. These two names immediately conjure up images of winning, of being at the very top of a chosen field.

And yet, it's important to recognize that you don't have to be the most influential person on this planet in order to use personal branding to your advantage. In fact, each and every day, your unique brand is 'out there' – representing you in any number of ways.

Just think about this for a moment.

What do you think people think about you? Be honest. And honesty means knowing the nice things that people say about you, as well as the not so nice.

You already do this every year in your organization, at performance appraisal time. So often such reviews are linked to money and that may not be the best time to think about personal branding.

You already do this every day in your relationships, as you communicate with other people – with your partner, your family and with absolutely everyone (yes, including that motorist who cut you up this morning, and that guy on the mobile phone on the train with the annoying laugh that you would like to strangle . . .).

And you already do this every moment as you communicate with yourself. Because what you think about, you are.

There are two complementary parts to personal branding: Reputation and Reach.

Reputation

'Reputation! Reputation! Reputation! Oh! I have lost my reputation. I have lost the immortal part of myself and what remains is bestial.'
Othello William Shakespeare (With thanks to Nick Hall)

In the course of each and every day you are an appalling parent, a wonderful partner, an amazing presenter, an invisible manager, etc, etc. These are all your behaviours, these are all you, and taken together, they will form others' perceptions of you. Over time, I hear you say. The odd mistake, raised voice or two-fingered gesture does not a brand make. Wrong.

As human beings we make up our minds about other people within the first few seconds of meeting them. We then subconsciously put them into one of our pigeon-holes, based on:

How they dress

Their facial features

How they move

How they speak

long before we have learned anything about them.

And first impressions are very powerful, and very hard to shift. Indeed, when we have made up our minds about someone, we then seek out evidence to support those first thoughts.

So, personal branding is about what others think of you, and what you think of yourself. Celebrity is simply an indication of the number of people who have heard of your name or brand.

Right now, you are a one-person walking, talking commodity that someone, somewhere, is passing judgement on.

Does that matter to you?

Of course it does. One of our main needs is to be liked – that's not respected, not believed, not necessarily loved, but liked.

And this is decided by you, in the following order:

Who you are

What you do

What you say

So, do you want to take control of your personal brand, or do you want your personal brand to take control of you?

As Peter Montoya, the world's number-one personal brand in personal branding, says: 'Imagine if you could influence how the leaders in your profession or company see you – as cutting-edge or conservative, a great listener or leader, and so on. That's what Personal Branding does. With a Personal Brand, others don't decide how you're perceived.

'You decide.'

That's power.

This gives you control over your reputation, one half of personal branding.

And if you decide you are here for a bigger purpose, or perhaps if you need to earn a living in a competitive marketplace, you will need to look at your:

Reach

Many people think this is about who you know. It isn't. It's about who knows you. Who you know is networking. Who knows you is reach.

How well known are you?

This does not mean how many people do you know, or know you personally. It means how many people have heard of your name and what do they associate it with?

Again, everyone will already have a certain reach, unless you live alone and never speak to anyone!

What can you do to take control of your reach?

The greater you decide your reach to be, the more of these you must do . . .

① Purpose

Decide on your private and public purpose. They may be the same, or at least complementary. Only share your private purpose with very trusted people, and only share your public purpose with the world.

THE NAKED LEADER EXPERIENCE

2 Presence

Treat everyone you meet with equal importance, making immediate rapport. They will like you if they feel you are showing them respect, and are interested in their number-one priority in the world, which is themselves.

3 Passion

When you think about what you do, and building a personal brand with reach, does your heart soar or sour? Be proud of what you do – when you speak with passion, enthusiasm and with massive energy people buy into your ideas, and you.

So, each and every day:

When you feel passionate, speak with total passion about what you do

And

When you feel down, and low, speak with total passion about what you do.

OK, those are three aspects of you, now for the critical one:

4 Profile

Like it or not, reach = high profile. You need people to see you, hear you and above all else, talk about you . . .

And be prepared for 'detractors' – the more you have, the more 'supporters' you have, and the more your awareness is growing.

Be prepared to be called 'big headed' or 'arrogant' – this doesn't mean that you should be either, but that is what you will be called by some people, usually because they are jealous.

Remember what Oscar Wilde said: 'There is **only one thing** in the world **worse than being talked** about, and that is not **being talked** about.'

And be prepared to be called 'mad' when you first embark on your adventure. These same people will call you 'lucky' when you succeed.

To raise your reach:

- **Speak at conferences.**

- **Attend local community meetings and have your say.**

- **Network – see _The Naked Leader_ or download at _www.nakedleader.com/integritybasednetworking_.**

- **Write a column in your chosen or target industry/sector journal, or in your in-company magazine.**

- **Attend social functions at work, and enjoy them!**

- **Write letters to newspapers (you will be amazed how many people read the letters pages).**

5 Partnerships

Find people already in the areas you want to be in and partner with them, learn from them and help them. Partnerships of this kind are all about quid pro quo. So be honest with a partner about what you need to achieve your dream, and ask them the same question – and help them with sincerity.

6 Precision

Focus everything you do on achieving your aims. Think about them every day. Yes, want them, but also reward yourself, and be thankful every time you take a step towards them. Remember, when you are clear about who you are and where you are going, life will conspire to help you.

7 Persistence

This is the deciding factor between success and failure in profile building and personal branding. There's enough about this, throughout this book!

One of the challenges in building a personal brand is the internal conflicts we feel, about who we are and why we are here.

'Me, Myself and I'
'Me.'

Who you really are, your true and authentic you – the highest version of your highest vision.

And below this ultimate level of identity, we all have two competing voices. The challenge is to be yourself while your ego (and other people's egos) is trying to make you like everyone else!

'My Self.'

The voice of calm certainty, that gently guides you on your true path – we know when we are hearing our selves when we feel ecstatic, as one, and at inner peace.

It will be your self that guides you to the life you were

born to lead. However, it never gets angry with you, or judges you, or punishes you – it sits patiently, waiting for you to reach your true path, and rewards you when you do by living every day in happiness and joy.

'I.'

'I' is the ego. Our egos are hungry to attract approval, but they never approve of others. Indeed, they take much of their energy from other people. The trouble is, your ego's feeling of satisfaction is short lived, so it's always hungry. Indeed, your ego's hunger can never be satisfied, and so its best lifelong compromise is to lie to you that the only way to be approved of, long term, is to be as much like other people as possible.

The ego is the part we show to the world; it is a false friend, a forgery of our true selves.

When we have to show, we are our egos.

When we know we know, we are our selves.

The ego is lost, when the self is found. The ego is without; the self is within.

If you wish to follow the chapters in the order they were written, please go to Chapter 3, on page 35.

are you a hero or a trailer?

Have you ever wondered what it'll be like to take centre stage?

Have you ever wondered what it'll be like to act in a multi-million-pound/dollar blockbuster? Well, I have news for you: you are the star in your own movie. This movie is simply called YOUR LIFE.

There is basically only one plot in all mainstream films, and it goes something like this.

The Hero's Quest

Hero is given a call to arms, he/she turns it down, and then it is offered again, turned down again; then again . . . this sequence goes on for a while, depending on the length of the film.

Finally the hero accepts their call to arms, they then enter 'the Road of Trials' – and the hero encounters numerous large/medium/small trials. Again, depending on the length of film they come through these and move forward towards their dream and outcome – their 'Pot of Gold'.

As they get nearer to the Pot, the challenges grow until just before it is achieved they get one or two humungous challenges, then they get their prize (there may be a final surprise trial just when we thought it was all over).

And if they have a sequel they do the same thing all over again, simply adding a 2 on the end!

And there we have it, the plot of almost every single mainstream film, and also the plot for life.

All of our lives. You and I are already somewhere on this journey. If you are seeking to be more in any aspect of your life you have accepted the call to arms and are now on the Hero's Quest. If you are totally content, have achieved everything you want and discovered inner peace then you may have found your Pot of Gold.

The rest of us are somewhere on the Road of Trials!

However, there are some differences. Let us imagine that we have written, and are starring in, such a story, and we have decided it will accurately reflect our lives.

We accept the call to arms, and start of the Road . . . we face our first challenge and with great belief and drama we overcome it. Then we face a bigger trial, and we, eh, we overcome that one as well, but only just. And then the trials get bigger, until one of two things happen:

● **We get 'stuck' in one.**

● **We give up.**

Life will keep teaching us a lesson until we learn it and move on. Have you noticed that if one area of your life goes wrong, it always goes wrong – the same thing over and over?

This is particularly true in the quest for the 'right' one to share our lives with – the finding of that special person.

So many people make prisons for themselves and their circumstances. The security they sought in marriage and family suddenly seems like Alcatraz. People escape, only to find freedom can be lonely – indeed, many people have been found swimming back to prison, because from the shore it can look like a luxury hotel compared to loneliness.

So, how exactly do we free ourselves from repeating the same mistakes over and over again?

We do something different – take a new approach.

And then there are those who give up, which is of course their choice.

So, a Hollywood film featuring most people would not be a blockbuster, as it would either last for ever (as we keep repeating the same mistakes) or be over in twenty minutes (if we give up).

But if we can keep going in this drama that is life, the analogy with movies becomes even more accurate. When we are nearing what we seek in life, our personal pot of gold, the trials and challenges can seem so much bigger.

Hollywood did not invent the concept of destiny. It realized it. The early pioneers of the cinema simply worked out how to use a movie camera to tell their tales; and they built an international industry to sell them.

The Hollywood model is the journey towards self-realization. This journey has its origins in the Greek legends of Herculean challenges and the tests of love undergone by Orpheus and other gods and earthly spirits.

These are all stories in which heroes conquer against the odds.

Christian martyrs and the Buddha likewise were important originators of the need to look inside in order to learn. Modern heroes like Mahatma Gandhi and Nelson Mandela fit this pattern, as role models for patience and endurance. Such universal spirituality is the bedrock of the popular 'feel-good' movie. It shows people that being strong within will lead them to lead others.

And so it is with our lives.

We are where we have come from, as a race, a community and as individuals. Your role, in taking control of your own destiny, is to choose how to describe your journey here. Look back over the last six years of your life. You will not remember every day-to-day experience – it will be key events, decisions and moments that stand out.

Think about it. What good fortune brought you here? What challenges did you face? If you had made different decisions on your Hero's Journey, would you now be on a completely different adventure, living a totally different life?

It is amazing how similar our lives and adventures are to movies and stories, although in real life there is no danger music, which is a shame as it would warn us of a new challenge approaching!

Purpose and Potential

I believe we are all born with a purpose, and the potential to achieve it. It may take us years to decide to go for it. When we do, that is the moment we begin our personal road of trials.

We know we are moving closer to our goal when the trials get bigger, and we see many people around us giving up – we keep going, over the last massive trial and achieve our pot of gold.

Possibly, like in James Cameron's *Titanic*, which follows this formula to the letter, our pot of gold is to die at peace. Perhaps there is no bigger reward in life than leaving this earth with no regrets, knowing we have fulfilled everything we could in our lives.

Let's look at you – when you were first conceived, you were a trailer. Imagine sitting in the cinema and watching a trailer for yourself, complete with American, gravelly voice-over: *Coming in nine months, or thereabouts, a new person for this earth, a person driven by emotions, by hope and fears, by pain and pleasures, and by love.*

And then you were born, one of the most amazing acts of nature. You were cut free to become the hero in your own adventure.

And so to now – your story may not yet be clear to you, but it began a while back and it has a long way to go before you reach your journey's end.

You will encounter pitfalls; make mistakes and many wrong turns. Everyone around you will comment on how you are doing. But they can only comment on how you fit in with their adventure, yours is yours, and yours alone.

In your life, you will get despondent and at times wish you had never started.

The merit of being in your own story is that you are aware of all this. You know that the darkest hour is just before dawn. When everything goes wrong and your plans collapse, you know that this means victory is just around the corner. Knowing this, you are able to keep your wits about you and ride the wave until you reach your destination.

And so now you can cast yourself in your own adventure – you write it, you direct it and you are the hero within it.

A question – what sort of movie are you starring in? Is it a comedy, a tragedy or a compelling drama of inspiration?

Some Inspirational Themes to Help on your Adventure

Theme	Movie
Loyalty	*Spartacus*
Seize the moment	*Dead Poets Society*
Discovering who you are and why you are here	*The Truman Show*
Coming home to self	*Breakfast at Tiffany's*
Helping others	*Pay It Forward* (the inspiration for *Just One Day*) *http://www.nakedleader.com/ content/justoneday/index.asp*
Good will prevail	*Excalibur*
Success can happen in a moment	*Gettysburg*
Reconciliation with your father	*Field of Dreams*
Helping others at great risk to yourself	*Schindler's List*
Pursue your dreams	*Billy Elliot*
Many realities	*Groundhog Day*
Persuasion and influence	*Twelve Angry Men*
Untapped potential within	*Good Will Hunting*
Success is whatever you want it to be	*Local Hero*
Persistence and self-belief	*Gladiator*
Belief	*The Legend of Bagger Vance*
Friendship	*The Shawshank Redemption*

The Definitive Leadership Film

If I was to ask you which film is widely regarded, and admired, for being THE definitive film on leadership, which film would you guess?

For Three Points:

Not only does it follow the Hero's Quest to the letter, and is one of the most popular films of all time, but almost every character reflects a real-life character-type.

For Two Points:

The leading character, S, is born to be king, however his evil uncle has other ideas, and kills S's father (and his brother), making it look like S's fault. Escaping to the wilds, S turns away from his destiny, until a guide persuades him to return, defeat evil and claim his birthright.

For One Point:

One of Disney's most popular animation films of all time, it has also been made into a stage musical. The twenty-minute sequence starting with Nala finding S (Simba) in the wilds, through to Simba deciding to return home, guided by Rafiki, is extraordinary, covering every leadership emotion.

(The answer can be found below, when reflecting the words in a mirror.)

The Lion King

If you wish to follow the chapters in the order they were written, please go to Chapter 21, on page 177.

the A–Z of being a naked leader . . .

Adventure	'Life is either a daring adventure, or nothing,' Helen Keller.
Birthright	Please tell everyone you know . . . that no matter what their age, their background or their present challenges, it is their birthright to be the very best that they already are, and to experience freedom, joy and inner peace in each and every moment. Ask them to tell everyone that they know, as this message is too important to keep to ourselves.
Choices	Forget change, think choice – and change will then happen.

Dreams	Help others' dreams come true, as often as you can.
Emotions	When you are feeling your very best, go out and be your best. When you are feeling your very worst, go out and be your best.
Focus	When you do the dishes, only do the dishes.
Giving	At the end of our lives, we would want to be remembered for the good that we have done.
Honesty	Put Truth, Trust and Teamwork high on your company's and team's agendas.
Imagination	Naked Leaders know that their people's imaginations are the last great untapped competitive weapon.
Just One Life	This is not a dress rehearsal – be the very best that you already are.
Knowing	Beyond Belief, and behind our internal (infernal) thoughts, we know how amazing we are. Sometimes, it can help to put our thoughts away.
Love	Everything we do as human beings, we do to move towards love, or move away from fear. Whichever we focus on, we move towards.
Meditation	Is becoming 'cool' again, hundreds of years after it was first written about, not too late, rather just in time.
Now	The only true time there is.
Ownership	Take full ownership of your life and everything that happens to you – take control of your own life before someone else does it for you.

THE NAKED LEADER EXPERIENCE

Peace	We are at peace the moment we are born, and then strive to rediscover this, the ultimate aim of every human being: inner peace.
Questions	So powerful and yet so under-used. Forget whether they are 'open', 'closed' or 'dynamic' – just ask more of them!
Reality	Take any event and ask, which one of these realities serves me/us best?
Self	We need to know, respect and value our selves before we can truly do the same with others. Our true selves radiate energy, our egos drain ours and others.
True Decision	The what we are going to achieve – we do not need to know the how yet, we just need to close off all other possible outcomes.
Unite	The future lies in uniting disparate individuals, acknowledging, valuing and welcoming our differences, while uniting as a force behind one vision.
Visible	Being present is being charismatic – be present in an age when remote communications are taking over.
Why?	There are 64 squares on a chessboard – most games are decided by who focuses best on the middle 4. Of the top 64 priorities in your life, which are the top 4?
X	That certain something true leaders possess – whatever it is, they/we are born with, or learn it, from within.

| You | Who are you, really? |
| Zest | Passion in all that we do, or why do it? |

As a Naked Leader you don't have to learn any of these, because you already know them – you just have to remember . . .

What I'm talking about is a game – a game that can't be won, only played. You've got a choice – you can stop, or you can start. Start walking – right back to where you've always been, and then stand there. Still. Real still. And remember – it was just a moment ago.

It is time for you to come out of the shadows. Time for you to choose. Now, play the game, the one that only you were meant to play – the one that was given to you when you came into this world. Are you ready?

The Legend of Bagger Vance
Screenplay by Jeremy Leven
Original book by Steven Pressfield

If you wish to follow the chapters in the order they were written, please go to Chapter 25, on page 209.

THE NAKED LEADER EXPERIENCE

the white rabbit

Take a look at your watch:

> Something you wear a lot
> Something you look at several times a day
> Something that you are very familiar with

Now, cover up the watch-face with your hand.
  Three quick questions:

Does your watch have numbers or roman numerals?

Does it have a second hand?

Can you describe the pattern on the face?

Time.

How often we see it, and how little we see it.

The only moment we live in is the present one.

Right now.

There's another one gone, and another one . . .

What's the time?

The time is now.

Time.

How often we tell it. How little we notice it. How seldom we live in it.

Time.

It gives all the evidence of being a constant, and yet it is not – scientists and academics have agreed for many years that it is totally relative.

What time is it?

It is now.

Alice sighed wearily. 'I think you might do something better with the time,' she sighed, 'than wasting it in asking riddles that have no answers.'

'If you knew time as well as I do,' said the Hatter, 'you wouldn't talk about wasting it. It's him.'

'I don't know what you mean,' said Alice.

'Of course you don't,' the Hatter said, tossing his head contemptuously. 'I dare say you never even spoke to Time!'

'Perhaps not,' Alice cautiously replied; 'but I know I have to beat time when I learn music.'

'Ah! That accounts for it,' said the Hatter. 'He won't stand beating. Now, if you only kept on good terms with him, he'd do almost anything you like with the clock.'

Alice in Wonderland
Lewis Carroll

If only

Can you imagine a world where we can actually take control of that most precious commodity, time?

We've been there, done that – taken control of time.

It hasn't worked.

Email promised us faster communication and reduced stress, as we were told it would enable us to take control of our communications.

And mobile phones – how they would make our lives so much easier.

And television. As a relaxant, it has taken over so many lives with its hypnotic powers.

Time.

If we could only control it, and make it work with us, not against us.

And just when we think we have time tamed, the white rabbit appears in our minds:

'Oh dear! Oh dear! I shall be too late!' He took a watch out of his waistcoat-pocket, and looked at it, and then hurried on.

Ibid

And you hear strange things about time, all the time: I was on a one-day time management conference. The trainer started by saying the conference promoters were running a competition, the first prize was one week in the Bahamas, all expenses paid. The good news was that to win you just had to give in your business card; the bad news was that the holiday started the day after the conference.

He asked for a show of hands on who would be able to

take the prize, if they won it. Out of over 500 people present, more than 400 put up their hands, including me.

The presenter then said: 'Sorry about that, guys, there is in fact no competition or trip to the Bahamas. But if over four hundred of you can take a week off at such short notice, then you have clearly got the time to sort out your time-management challenges.'

A very powerful lesson to us all.

Another example of our use of time came via the radio. One programme I tuned into was inviting people to call or text to say what they would do if they had an extra thirty minutes each and every day.

Doesn't sound like much, does it? And yet the calls and texts flooded in with people's dreams of how they would spent their extra thirty minutes.

If only we had thirty minutes in our lifetimes, to do what we choose!

That's one episode of *Coronation Street*.

Time – it can either help us or hinder us.

And it is totally relative.

Compare the following two situations and tell me if time passes equally in each:

● **When you are with a loved one.**

● **When you are in the dentist's chair.**

Of course not. In the first one, time flies. And in the second, time draaaaaaaaaaaaaags.

Time is not an absolute, it is relative.

So, how can we take control of time?

Simple, we need to spend time in it.

THE NAKED LEADER EXPERIENCE

How?

Focus on the present – the now – this very moment. Do it now.

The present is the only moment you ever live in. How seldom you experience it in all its glory. You are usually too busy worrying about something that has already happened, which we cannot change, or something that may happen in the future, to stop and focus on the right now.

And yet, when you do this, it is one of the most enlightening experiences in the world.

Look around you right now – hear the sounds, see – really see – the people, the sights of nature. Put all other thoughts out of your mind, and be in the very present, truly at one with yourself, the world and everything in it.

When we pay total and absolute attention to the present moment and what we are doing in it, it is an amazing experience.

Time seems to expand.

Also, think about time in relation to your worries and fears. If aliens were to visit our planet, they would have such a laugh, and report back to their spaceship or planet: *Indeed these human beings are a very strange grouping. They seem to have forgotten that time is now, and spend most of their thinking in the past and in the future! They worry, a lot, about life, but the illogical thing is what they worry about most. They worry about things that have happened to them in the past, which they have absolutely no control over and can never change, and they worry about things that have not yet happened, and what could go wrong! It is no wonder happiness eludes so many of these people.*

Focus on what you are doing, whatever it may be, on

what is happening around you, for 100 per cent and time will slow for you – and be in ever greater supply.

You will begin to feel like the human being that you are, and less like the human doing that you have become.

Try living a time-free day:

Choose a day when you have no appointments. Take down or cover all clocks the night before . . .

Wake up when you wake up – not when told to do so by any alarms.

Get up when you want to.

And then live, in every moment.

Eat when you are hungry.

Do what you want, when you want.

If you feel tired, have a lie down.

If you feel energized, go for a walk.

Go to bed when you want.

The day will seem to go very fast – almost too fast!

And yet you will feel you have achieved so much more.

Quite apart from feeling relaxed and refreshed, you will feel in total control.

When we start to work with time – and don't always feel as if time is 'against us' – we stop existing and start living.

Look at your children, and how fast they seem to grow. The only time most people realize how fast, is when they are not children any more, and then it is too late to enjoy, to really enjoy, being with them as they grow. Remember: every moment your child is with you is a moment to cherish.

Balance
Our use of time is one of the main factors that puts us out of balance.

The whole discussion on work/life balance is about how much time we spend physically and thinking about each.

I don't know about you, but these scales really scare me:

● **They imply that when I am 'working', I am not 'living' – indeed, the two are in direct opposition to each other.**

● **Looking at our lives as a set of scales has an inherent time conflict in itself.**

● **Replacing 'life' with 'home' makes it worse. It gives us an immediate conflict – if I spend too much time doing one thing – work – my entire life is out of balance.**

Oh dear!

I wish these scales had some kind of measurement. When I made this comment to a stress 'expert' at a conference, she said that we tend to spend one third of our lives at work, one third asleep and one third enjoying ourselves.

I'm SORRY?!

What a depressing thought! Who said we couldn't enjoy ourselves at work?

Time – take control of it before it takes any more control of you.

Because how you feel in the moment, in any given moment, is all that's important. You are as 'balanced' as you feel right now, wherever you are and whatever you are doing.

Cats know true and total balance; they truly live in the moment.

I bought my first cat in 1987. Possum turned out to be the most gentle, caring, loving friend anyone could ever ask for. He would sit on my bed, listening to my stories of leadership, of the amazing people I was meeting, and most of all keeping me company as I wrote. He would sleep beside me, and when he stretched onto the keyboard to produce what looked like gobbledegook, he was telling me to take a break and give him a cuddle.

It's not just balance, one learns so much about leadership from cats, about persistence (he once fell out of an upstairs window, onto a bush, brushed himself off and returned upstairs to sleep – I had to race ahead to close the window before he did it again!), about persuasion and, most of all, about kindness.

Possum died while I was writing this book, on Monday, 9 June 2003 at 11.10 a.m., peacefully, aged 16½ years.

He was always there when I needed him, he would sit in my lap for hours, and no matter what happened, he gave us all total, unconditional love.

Goodbye, Possum, we love you, and always will.

If you wish to follow the chapters in the order they were written, please go to Chapter 13, on page 107.

THE NAKED LEADER EXPERIENCE

nightwake!

Please read this chapter with an open mind.

And as you do so, you will discover the most amazing development in leadership and self-discovery.

It's the hottest thing in personal development, and it is so, so powerful. When you have finished this single chapter you will know how to take total and absolute control of an extra third of your life.

Because we spend about one third of our lives asleep.

Imagine if you could do this, under your own control, when you are asleep!

Well, you can. Welcome to the world of lucid dreaming.

At the moment it's seen as a personal development/ mind-body-spirit phenomenon; however it's heading mainstream fast.

Lucid dreaming is simply this: the ability to realize when

you are dreaming, to experience that dream with all of your senses, and to guide your dreams in whatever direction you choose.

What has this to do with leadership, success and personal development/discovery?

1. **If you sometimes feel shy or nervous with other people, speak to them and be with them without any fears or worry in your dreams. The response will come directly from the pools of deep knowledge within their minds. The dreamer has only to wait for it and listen.**

2. **Imagine if you simply could not fail – what would you do? Where would you go? Who would you be? If you are not ready to ponder this power question in real life, do it first in your dreams!**

3. **If you have a fear, of anything – in your dreams you can experience being without that fear.**

4. **Open up your ideas, innovation and imagination. Get those creative juices flowing, and flying! We already have access to everything we need, to be anything we want, and lucid dreaming accelerates that process.**

5. **In your dream, go to a place of total peace and calm, a perfect state, and ask yourself who you are and why you are here. We can put ourselves in any healing and relaxing situations that we choose, and it is all totally personal and private.**

6. **Connect, or reconnect, with someone you love, at a deep level, perhaps as a dress-rehearsal for doing so in real life.**

Ask questions, or share feelings that perhaps you have not done for a while.

7 Before an important event, imagine living through that event in advance, everything happening perfectly, like a dream. Never has the phrase 'sleep on it' had such meaning!

8 Imagine reconciling yourself with someone from your past or your present – make peace and feel at peace.

9 See where you want to go, and who you want to be. See that perfect you, feel how special you are and connect with the awesome powers and abilities you have within you, right now.

10 Meet with your favourite characters from fiction – indeed, many people I know have fictional mentors. I have one whom I meet whenever I choose. Interact with them and draw upon their power.

11 Experience the awesome feelings of flying. And as you do so, enjoy seeing the world in which you live and help connect yourself with it, and with all people, everywhere.

12 Solve a problem: in dreams we have direct access to our subconscious minds. No time is wasted worrying that we cannot find the answer to a particular problem.

13 Sports improvement: play the sport – golf, tennis, whatever you choose – in your mind. Previous squash champions have done this – hitting the ball up and down a wall for hours. Seeing it happen perfectly and consistently has proved to bring enormous improvements in performing.

14 Adventure: we all seek, need and enjoy an adventure in our lives – now you can have one of your own design.

15 Learn a new skill – if you are learning to play the piano, or speak a new language, practise in your dream – it can be a lot more fun than practising in real life!

16 Well-being: the effects of visual imagery on the body are well established. Just as practice in a dream can enhance your waking performance, healing dream imagery may well improve your physical health.

17 Transcendence: lucid dreaming clearly demonstrates the astonishing fact that the world we see is a construct of our mind. This concept, so elusive when sought in waking life, is the cornerstone of spiritual teachings. It forces us to look beyond everyday experience and ask, 'If this is not real, what is?' Not only does lucid dreaming lead us to question the nature of reality, but for many it is also a source of transcendent experience. Exalted and ecstatic states are common in lucid dreams.

I could go on and on. But I won't, because by now you are convinced, nearly convinced or not convinced at all.

And that's fine, because you don't have to believe, to experience lucid dreams – and if you don't like it the first time, choose not to do so again.

Now, like most things in life, because lucid dreaming takes time, we need to allocate the time for it.

So, please have your diary at the ready.

Hmmm – you look very busy in the next couple of weeks. What about at night?

What are your plans between, say, midnight and 2 a.m., and then again between about 4 and 6 a.m.?

Oh, you will be asleep.

Excellent.

I jest, of course.

Because unlike most things in life, you can experience lucid dreaming whenever you sleep. And everyone sleeps. Or nods off.

And everyone dreams, even if you have never remembered a single dream, you have had them.

If you haven't, then you're dead. And if you are dead, with all due respect, you are probably not reading this right now.

Between midnight and 2 a.m., and then again between about 4 and 6 a.m. are the most frequent times that we dream – or, put another way, around an hour after falling asleep, for two hours, and again in the two hours before we awake.

OK, OK. I hear you.

Whatever you feel right now, you are asking me the same question: 'Come on, David, tell me . . . how do I do it?'

OK.

This is the how – and because you won't have to wade through all of the massive tomes that are now being written on lucid dreaming, I am saving you a fortune in your most precious commodity, time.

On the next page alone you will see three words, a question.

Photocopy them.

Or write them on a card – perhaps the back of your business card, or someone else's!

Make sure it is on something you can carry around with you all day, discreetly, wherever you go.

ARE YOU
DREAMING?

Now, ask yourself this question, often, each and every day. At least a dozen times, ideally twenty. You can do this privately; the key is that it becomes a habit, a part of your daily routine, so that the question will crop up in your dream.

So, ask yourself right now: Are You Dreaming?

The answer will probably be: I don't know.

Because our minds cannot tell the difference between something we imagine with emotional intensity and something we experience in 'reality', we don't know.

Move to the next stage: Find out.

By doing the following:

1 Read the question again.

In dreams, letters and words become jumbled, and so when you read the question a second time, if it reads the same – i.e. 'Are You Dreaming?' – the answer is no.

If you are reading these words and they make sense, you are indeed awake.

Now, if those three words appear strange in any way – upside down, or jumbled up – at any time you look at them, you may be dreaming.

However, you may also be drunk.

So we need to do a second check.

2 Jump off the ground and fly.

No, you read that correctly.

Unless you are on the moon as you read this, when you are awake and you jump up, off the ground, with both feet, you will land back on the ground again after reaching perhaps six inches off the ground.

Good stuff – thanks to Isaac Newton we call that 'gravity'.

But if you find that you are floating upwards to touch the ceiling, you may be dreaming.

If the three-word question changes each time you look at it and you float up to the ceiling, you are probably dreaming.

One final check. But just before that, a key point. Go with the flow, respect what is happening to you and what you are doing. Do not try to control it, and do not let it go.

Find the perfect balance in between – enjoy the experience without analysing it. Because when we analyse something our conscious mind slips in.

And lucid dreaming happens with our subconscious mind, and the moment we begin to think too hard, or control, or analyse, we simply wake up.

And at the other extreme, if we just say to ourselves fine, and let go of this three-step process, we are very likely to go off and have our dream without realizing we are having it – dream normally.

Both of which are fine, I am only offering you a third option.

And the third stage of the three-step process is:

3 Go and lean against a wall.

If you are awake, you will touch the wall with your hand, and it will support your whole body weight.

If you are asleep, you may find yourself 'falling' through the wall.

As you may not know whether you are awake or asleep, look at the wall and expect it to move – wait and see what happens.

Now, knowing that as you read this you are awake, I will carry on as if you are asleep!

Because you are now at the beginning of your lucid dream.

And now, go with the flow, respect the dream (by which you are respecting your self) and enjoy.

For further information, check out the Lucidity Institute, one of the most respected and informed websites on lucid dreaming, at *http://www.lucidity.com*

If you are reading this between 2004 and 2006, this will be pioneering.

If you are reading this after 2006, it will be well known.

If you are reading it after 2008, lucid dreaming will be mainstream.

With thanks to Igor Ledochowski.

When we lucid dream we are fearless, if only we could do this every day in our waking lives:

> *Dance like no-one's watching you,*
> *Love like you've never been hurt,*
> *Sing like no-one is listening,*
> *Live like heaven on earth.*

If you wish to follow the chapters in the order they were written, please go to Chapter 34, on page 293.

a deeper still

A few words on stress . . .

That's quite enough, thank you.

More than enough has been written about stress. It's time to look for some antidotes and some structured relaxation.

Now, this book is all about choices, so I am going to offer seven different ways to achieve perfect relaxation, inner peace and a deeper still.

Also, as I am sharing with you how to do these things, I'm avoiding all the jargon that normally surrounds them. Such hype can normally fill a book, I don't want to do that, I want you to feel calm, centred and relaxed.

Oh, and unlike most 'lists' in this book, they are not in any order, although I can vouch for every one of these.

Beginning with this incredibly simple, yet powerful exercise:

1 **Structured Relaxation**

Time: 30 minutes

What to do:

● **Find a very quiet room.**

● **Lie down, ideally on a mattress on the floor, although any-where comfortable will do.**

● **Cover yourself with a thin blanket, or duvet cover.**

● **Keeping your eyes open, focus on your breathing.**

● **Breathe deeper.**

● **Clear your mind of any and all thoughts. (They may creep back in. If they do, gently clear them away).**

What will happen?

After anything between 5 and 20 minutes, you will feel an incredible, warm glow throughout your body.

When it begins just continue to focus on your breathing and allow its energy to flow through you.

Personal Experience

My first experience – Bristol, 1990, and as I lay there I thought I had been conned. And after 15 minutes, with my facilitator next to me, I thought, Oh well, I may as well go for it. Seconds later I felt incredible warmth radiate through me and a sense of well-being soon followed.

2 Above the Stars

Time: 60 minutes

What to do:

- Lie outside on a clear, cloudless evening or night.

- Look at the stars – respect their greatness, and imagine that you are absorbing some of their power.

- Look only at the stars.

- Now, turn the universe upside down – and imagine that the stars are below you. You are floating above them but are held to your garden, and the earth, by a massive magnet. You are safe.

- It may take some time, it may happen fast.

- When you are ready, reverse the stars again, lie back, breathing deeply before you get up.

Personal Experience

This happened to me on the fourth attempt. Many people had told me about doing this – so I persevered. Suddenly on the fourth time it was as if I was holding up the whole world, and about to fall onto the stars. It didn't actually relax me, but it certainly made the world and the stars, and me I suppose, seem awesome.

3 For You and a Partner – Storybook Reunion

Time: as long as you both choose

What to do:

- Take down your barriers, and agree to do this.

- Arrange a rendezvous – one at which you used to meet when you first got to know each other.

- Travel to the rendezvous separately.

- Meet up – as if it is for only the first or second time.

- Take special time to look at each other – into each other's eyes, minds and souls. Smile and remember. Hold each other if you both choose. See everyone else around you disappear from your sight.

- And then, do whatever you like, this is your private and shared moment.

Personal Experience

My wife Rosalind and I used to meet under the clock at Waterloo, and this we did again, both travelling independently. A very private afternoon of rediscovery, in a very public place – London!

4 Visit a Church

Time: as long as you choose

What to do:
Note: You do not have to be religious for this to work.

THE NAKED LEADER EXPERIENCE

- **Visit a church – when it is quiet.**

- **It does not matter what denomination it is, or your beliefs.**

- **Simply sit quietly, alone or with another – and be at one with all that surrounds you, the magnificent sights, sounds and smells.**

- **Respect everyone who is there, as they will respect you.**

- **Make a small donation on your way in or out.**

Personal Experience

I walked into a Russian Orthodox church, where services are frequent, almost continuous. Once I realized I was welcome I sat there in awe. I did not have a clue what was going on but by respecting those involved, they respected me.

5 Do Nothing

Time: set a specific time

What to do:

- **Choose to do nothing whatsoever.**

- **Veg-out completely – do absolutely nothing.**

- **Do not get bored or irritated, just allow time to pass, as it would do if you were there or not.**

Personal Experience

This isn't easy, but it's worth the effort. I first sat at a bus stop, doing nothing, however I found myself dreading the bus would arrive and interrupt, which it did! So I went for a walk and found a bench in the middle of Rome, and sat there, doing nothing. It was magic. The noises around me – the bustle of life – evaporated.

6 Listen to Music

Time: however long the music lasts

What to do:

● Listen to music – ideally on headphones.

● Close your eyes and really listen.

● I mean really listen, and as you listen, see the band, the singer or the orchestra.

● Focus on every note, every instrument and every variation.

7 Let go of a burden

There were two Buddhist monks walking along a river bank in the heat of the day. As they walked they could not help but notice a woman struggling in the water. She was in obvious difficulty.

The older of the two waded into the water, which came to chest height, lifted the woman above the water and carried her out to the bank. There he set her down and checked that she was all right.

After a very short while the monks continued on their way without saying more about the incident until, on the fifth day, the younger monk could contain himself no longer and said, 'You touched a woman! Why aren't you speaking about this or doing anything about it? We're Buddhist monks – you're not supposed to touch women at all. You know that.'

The older monk said, 'Yes. I touched her. I picked her up and carried her for five minutes – but,' he added, 'you've carried her for five whole days . . .'

With thanks to Naomi Langford-Wood

Sometimes 'letting go' can mean coming home:
I said I understood, and touched his arm.

We stood slightly closer. He was crying.

I waited, and would have waited for ever.

Telling him without telling him, that I was ready to listen and that whatever he told me was fine.

He said it again: 'I can't go home.'

'I know,' I said – a few years ago I would have asked someone, in the same position, 'Why?' and ignited their emotions.

So this time I said, and said again: 'I know.'

And this time he answered the question I did not ask.

Through his tears he said, 'Because I wouldn't know what to say to her. We've lost our way. Fourteen years of marriage and we've lost it. We can't speak to each other any more; we just live in the same house. We exist together.'

(Pause.)

He carried on – 'I can't go home – I wouldn't know what to say.'

And then I asked him a question, I hoped it was the right one: 'If you did know what to say, what would it be?'

He looked at me and smiled, the first smile in over an

hour. He knew what I was up to, he knew the power of the question I was asking.

He mocked me, in a warm and friendly way: 'Oh, Mr Taylor, if I did know what to say, I would say it, but I don't know what to say, so I won't be saying anything.'

(Pause.)

Total change of state and emotion – a different choice made deep within.

'And if I did know what to say, I would hold her close to me, and I would look her in the eyes and say I love you, and ask her if she would spend the rest of her life with me. And I would tell her my hopes, my fears and my dreams.'

And then he stopped and simply walked away.

He walked home, and said what he said . . .

That was six months ago, a true story, repeated with permission but no names needed, because it could be anyone who has been with someone for a while, and lost sight of what it is like to really be with them. And so many people wait until it is too late.

And he said to me a few weeks later:

'If you love someone, tell them, and love them, like it was your last ever day together, because that day will come.'

If you wish to follow the chapters in the order they were written, please go to Chapter 20, on page163.

THE NAKED LEADER EXPERIENCE

how to lose weight

Burn off more energy than you consume.
 And that's it.

*(Don't tell anyone – this is clearly a big secret, made very
complex by diet books and some food manufacturers!)*

Book Two

Reignite Your Relationships

business brilliance

You and your people are your next big idea.

Everything you need, to be anything you want, lies waiting within you and them.

And yet traditional ways of so-called strategy and the releasing of ideas have not worked:

- **They are only discussed and agreed to at an intellectual level.**

- **They are boring! Usually indicated more by yellow Post-It® Notes than by decisive action!**

- **They take too long – often several months – to agree.**

- **They are rarely bought into at a deep, emotional, passionate level.**

The only way – the only single way – to make lasting change in any person or organization is to buy into that change at an emotional level. Understanding where we are going at an intellectual level is simply not enough. We have to feel passion, excitement, a sense of adventure, if we are to make lasting change.

Why should companies put up with having boring missions, aims and goals, when they can have a destiny?

Life is either a daring adventure, or nothing.
Helen Keller

In addition, in today's fast business world we simply do not have the luxury of deciding our journey, and destination, in months or even weeks – we have to decide it in days. Any company that can do this quickly, with a common desired future reality, a destiny, will be in an awesomely powerful position to master their own future.

None of the traditional approaches will deliver this – it is time for something totally different.

The best way, indeed the only way, to predict the future, is to shape it.

The only way people can truly buy into the future is to see it, touch it and feel it.

In effect, to experience it before it happens. This is achieved using guided visualization. Such techniques of seeing the future are not new; they are widely used in sports psychology and in individual one-to-one coaching and mentoring.

Nothing is beyond your reach when you use guided visualization. The very act of 'dreaming' your desires wakes up your subconscious mind, stretches your imagination and innovation, and ignites a new fire and

THE NAKED LEADER EXPERIENCE

energy within you, that makes you unstoppable.

Your subconscious mind cannot tell the difference between what you have experienced and what you have experienced with emotional intensity. That's why we can 'live' the experience of a horror film even though we know it is fiction, or feel ourselves delivering a major presentation at work, even though it has not yet happened. We can even remember at a deep emotional level our dreams, even though they are not really happening to us in this real world.

The most powerful and influential part of Business Brilliance is that it can be applied to any single desired reality – a new global destiny for a company, a project outcome for a team, or for any activity.

Right now, please close your eyes and imagine taking your company, project or team to achievements they have never experienced before. Imagine seeing a more ambitious future and knowing you can make it happen. Above all, imagine liberating all of those ideas within your people.

That is only a brief glimpse of what you can do with your people.

How?

Away from the office, in a conference room:

- **Set the scene for the session, and build trust, by explaining that this is a structured relaxation session and will be an enjoyable experience which happens to be hundreds of years old!**

- **Ask people to make themselves comfortable on the floor – ideally with a pillow.**

- **Invest in a meditation/relaxation tape or CD (there are many on the market) and play it.**

- **Before they relax ask them to clear their minds, and when they are relaxed, to see, feel and think about the future of their dreams, for the project, team and company.**

- **Do the session.**

- **When it is completed ask everyone to write down any and every idea/thought that came to them.**

With a team of, say, twelve, you will end up with over 100 ideas.

Then, prioritize these ideas on the basis of which will give the biggest impact to the issues you are facing. Do this by asking the team which few ideas stand out as outstanding.

The belief that we have to look outside of our teams, companies and our selves for new ideas is well stoked by many consultancies, who claim to have a monopoly on new ideas! They do not. You may not realize it, but everything you need to be anything you want is already within you and your people.

In 1957 in Bangkok, a group of monks had to relocate their massive, ten and a half foot tall, 2.5-ton clay Buddha from their temple to a new location to make way for a new highway being built through the city. They used a crane to lift the idol, but it began to crack, and then rain began to fall. The head monk was concerned about damage to the sacred Buddha, and he decided to lower the statue down to the ground and cover it with a large canvas tarp to protect it from the rain.

Later that evening, the monk went to check on the Buddha. He shined a flashlight under the tarp, and noticed a gleam reflected through a crack in the clay. Wondering about what he saw, he got a chisel and hammer, and began to chip away at the clay. The gleam turned out to be gold, and many hours later the monk found himself face to face with an extraordinary, huge solid-gold Buddha.

Historians believe that several years before this, the Burmese army was about to invade Thailand, then called Siam. The monks covered their precious statue with an 8-inch layer of clay to disguise its value. Very likely the Burmese slaughtered all the Siamese monks, and the secret of the statue's golden essence remained intact until that day in 1957.

We are all like the golden Buddha, in some way. We are covered with a protective layer, often so well covered that we have forgotten how to remember our true value.

With thanks to Jack Canfield

If you wish to follow the chapters in the order they were written, please go to Chapter 10, on page 87.

let's get naked!

You may know the story of the Emperor's New Clothes – of how a king paid some deceitful tailors to kit him out in the most wonderful costumes, and how he was tricked into wearing nothing by being told that only very intelligent people could actually see the garments!

It was a child who first shouted out from the crowd as the king passed by, looking very regal, naked and also probably very cold!

Everyone else was cheering, pretending to see the fine clothes on the king, because to admit they could see nothing was to admit they were stupid.

How often do we dress ourselves up in such emperor's clothes, so we can impress other people, win their approval and acceptance?

The great irony here is that when we get 'naked', we no

longer seek or hunger for these, because we attract them, automatically, because of who we are, not what we are 'wearing' or, more accurately, what we are pretending to 'wear'.

So, let's get naked and ask ourselves one question.

How do we judge how we are doing?

So often, we judge it, and our success, not by our own criteria, but by how we are doing compared to others.

Actually, that is what I used to believe, and it was a very destructive idea.

I now believe we judge our success not by how we are doing compared to others, but how we **think** we are doing, compared to others.

Even more destructive.

We do it in our personal lives, in our teams compared to other teams inside the same organization, and as organizations, 'benchmarking' against other companies.

It is crazy, and destructive, and so very human. Because we all want one thing, above all else: we want to be valued, especially by our peers.

How can we do things differently?

On a personal level success is yours to define, and yours alone. This may indeed mean a certain sum of money, a career or a bigger home. Or it could be a relationship, putting up our son's train set or simply cooking a meal without third-party help.

Success, true success, comes from within.

And if you believe that worrying what other people think of you will change the way they think about you, then you are living on a different planet in an entirely different solar-system.

THE NAKED LEADER EXPERIENCE

To laugh often and much; to win the respect of intelligent people and the affection of children; to earn the appreciation of honest critics and endure the betrayal of false friends; to appreciate beauty, to find the best in others; to leave the world a little better; whether by a healthy child, a garden patch or a redeemed social condition; to know even one life has breathed easier because you have lived. This is the meaning of success.

Ralph Waldo Emerson

So, decide what success means for you, and acknowledge that everyone else has the birthright to decide what success means for them.

Then you can truly know your self, and know how to help others, from within.

Indeed, if you will pardon the expression, let's get naked with those around us!

With your partner, perhaps of several years, with maybe the spark of love fading, think and act on the words of Christopher Morley:

If one were given five minutes' warning before sudden death, five minutes to say what it all meant to us, every telephone booth would be occupied by people trying to call up other people to stammer that they loved them.

Why wait? Go tell them now. Your final day together will come.

And let's get naked with our boss (heaven forbid!) – let's speak openly and honestly, and stop hiding behind all of the façades we put up before us.

Who will you get naked with?

If you had three wishes, right now, one for yourself, one for your family and one for your team or company, what would they be?

Put this book down wherever you are, close your eyes and open your mind, your thoughts and your imaginations.

Welcome back, if you have actually come back, because when we open up our hearts and our true selves to these wishes, we glow with energy.

We put aside our 'emperor's clothes' – the destructive learning that we can be little more that what we have become, the false knowledge that we do not have all that we need inside us, and most of all the hungry ego that goes out seeking approval each and every day.

And there is plenty of success to go around, because your wishes will be yours, and different from other people's.

Why obsess yourself with how well you are doing compared to others?

The only question that matters is this: how are you doing now compared to where you want to go, and who you want to be?

And the ultimate irony of wanting to be liked, valued and respected is this. When you truly understand, know and respect your self, you will treat others differently – you will listen to them, be more open to acknowledge different opinions to your own, and be more able to help them achieve their dreams.

Because you would have put your 'emperor's clothes' away, for ever.

Nasrudin was refused entry to a dinner at the Dorchester, despite his invitation, because his clothes were not

THE NAKED LEADER EXPERIENCE

deemed suitable. He returned within the hour, resplendently dressed, and was guided to his table with all respect and deference. When the meal began however, he began behaving in a very strange manner. He poured the soup down the front of his shirt, he smeared butter on his sleeves and he rubbed his main course into his jacket. Finally, all the very English restraint that surrounded him was broken.

'What are you doing?' said the man opposite, and every-one craned (not too obviously) to hear the answer.

'Well, it seems that my clothes are the ones that were welcome here, rather than me, so I don't see why they shouldn't also share the benefit of this sumptuous meal.'

Thanks to Bill Parslow

You are already perfect

What are you looking for when you go to the store and spend money that you may not have?

Who are you trying to find when you go to the car show-room and see a car you can't quite afford, but the little voice in your head says, People will think better of you. Who are you trying to impress? The big house, the fancy holidays, the expensive jewellery, all these things will carry much more value if you truly view YOUR SELF as the price-less possession.

You are already perfect.

I do believe that financial wealth is something worth striving for, as long as you understand that it is the cream on the cake and not the cake itself. In today's world money does serve a purpose, but so does your spirit. And I come across so many people who are geared up just for financial, tangible wealth and neglect the feeling of wealth spiritual calmness, happiness and wholeness can bring. If only we could attain balance. We place such a high value on things money can buy, and neglect to see that the real value can be found in the things that we are given for free.

Life.

If we have the misfortune of bumping our vehicle, we can replace it. If our home gets broken into and some of our material belongings get taken, while annoying, we can replace those too. But have you tried replacing your life. Without which, the car and the home have no meaning. You are already perfect. When was the last time you looked into your partner's eyes and were awestruck? Nobody in the world has eyes like him or her. Your partner, family, friends are all original pieces of art that should be marvelled at every day. We get so used to seeing 'expensive' art in frames, that we forget to notice the price-less art that is all around us. You are already perfect.

When was the last time you lay on your back and gave due consideration to how your subconscious brain keeps your heart pumping blood around the body? Your heart is made of a special type of muscle that doesn't become fatigued. Each heartbeat that we feel in our chest is one complete contraction and relaxation of the heart muscle. The right side of the heart collects blood carrying waste carbon dioxide from the body, and pumps it to the lungs. The left side collects blood with fresh oxygen from the lungs and pumps it around the body. Your heart is the engine that keeps your body going. Every day this vital organ beats about 100,000 times, pumping the equivalent of 2,000 gallons of blood . . . and you don't even think about it! You see, I'm right. You are already perfect. If this is something you can do without 'thinking', imagine the things you can achieve when you set your mind to achieving a particular result.

The cars, the homes, the high-powered jobs, the expensive clothes and jewellery are great. Just don't put too much emphasis on them. For if you make these things WHO you are, then what happens if you lose them? Do you not risk losing your perfect self in the process? Why risk that when you are already perfect?

Peace, love and light.

Steve Rock
www.therock.com

If you wish to follow the chapters in the order they were written, please go to Chapter 37, on page 313.

seven degrees of synergy

*We, humanity, are on this planet together, and we have to share this world, because we **are** sharing this world.*

Your Inner Journey to the Real
Janice Duthac

We are all connected. Because we are all connected, everyone is closer than we may think.

This is why computer viruses can reach millions of people in minutes.

This is why real viruses are so difficult to control, as we saw with SARS in 2003.

At a more local level, this is why the grapevine in organizations is so effective.

And mobile phones and radios play a part as well.

On the final day of the 2002–3 football season in Scotland, it went right down to the last ninety minutes.

Rangers have to win at home. Celtic have to win away. Celtic have to win by more goals than Rangers to win the championship. I watched both games on two separate televisions. How long would it take a goal from one game to reach the fans at the other – as indicated by the general buzz, or silence, that the news would bring?

Rangers conceded a goal, the Celtic fans cheered in . . . 8 seconds. Celtic missed a penalty, Rangers knew they had won the championship in . . . 4 SECONDS!

And in everyday life, in business and in our personal lives, we are all connected to everyone else, every second of every day.

You may have heard of Six Degrees of Separation: through just six intermediaries, you are linked to everyone in the world. It is the notion behind what has been dubbed the small world effect. And this so-called small world effect is turning out to have some pretty big consequences, and it is one of the hottest topics in science.

Many people believe it could revolutionize the way we think about everything from economic crashes to global-ization. And not just with communication, with ideas as well.

Malcolm Gladwell coined the phrase 'the tipping point' and wrote a book by the same name. He argued that ideas, brands, products and companies 'tip' when they reach a state of common parlance – when enough people have heard of something, and are telling enough other people, that they will become a part of normal, every day conversation.

In recent years many things have tipped:

- **Google, the search engine.**

- **Friends Reunited in the UK, and similar websites around the world.**

- **Michael Moore's book, *Stupid White Men*, tipped because librarians got together and decided the book was too important not to be published properly.**

And *The Tipping Point* book tipped as well!

So, with all of this synergy and connection, why are we so nasty to each other?

One reason is that we feel detached from each other, as individuals, groups and communities. This detachment is of our own making.

One evening at Frankfurt airport, while waiting for my flight, I walked around and looked at all of the people flying to so many different destinations. I wondered if I could tell the destination country, or even hemisphere, just by looking at those people waiting to journey there.

I could not!

Moscow, Sydney, New York, Cape Town, and many others, my success rate at guessing was zero, each group of people could have been flying anywhere.

And that is when I suddenly realized, there is no 'us and them', there is only 'us and us'.

And we can begin to feel this by moving just one stage beyond Six Degrees of Separation, to Seven Degrees of Synergy.

The seventh degree happens when we help others through acts of kindness. It may be surprising our partner; it may be helping a friend, or carrying out a random act of kindness.

Random Acts of Kindness

*'Life's most persistent and urgent question is: what are you
doing for others?'*
Martin Luther King

You are invited to carry out a random act of kindness. As
often as you wish, in all that you do . . .

- **Once a day.**

- **Once a week.**

- **Once a month . . .**

A random act of kindness is helping another person, or
another team in your company or community, or any
group of people other than yourself.

Examples are endless, including:

- **Spending time with someone who is lonely, or who lives
  alone, and caring for the frail and infirm.**

- **Listening – paying 100 per cent attention – to your partner
  and your children.**

- **Taking time to find out who lives next door to you, either
  side, and offering to help in any way you can.**

- **Buying food for a homeless person, and giving them just
  five minutes of your time (it's not scary – just ask, 'How are
  you doing?').**

- Sending flowers to a loved one when it is not an anniversary, birthday or Mother's Day, etc.

- Speaking highly of people, to their face and behind their backs – and making any criticism constructive.

- On the road – letting a car out of a junction (e.g. turning right or reversing out of their home).

- Giving your spare change to charity.

- Taking a genuine interest in other people – respecting their values and opinions.

Over to you, and please remember, next time you pass someone who needs your help: it is very easy to be cynical; it is far more rewarding to take action.

The Starfish Story

Once upon a time, there was a wise man who used to go to the ocean to do his writing. He had a habit of walking on the beach before he began his work.

One day, as he was walking along the shore, he looked down the beach and saw a human figure moving like a dancer. He smiled to himself at the thought of someone who would dance to the day, and so, he walked faster to catch up.

As he got closer, he noticed that the figure was that of a young man, and that what he was doing was not dancing at all. The young man was reaching down to the shore, picking up small objects and throwing them into the ocean.

He came closer still and called out, 'Good morning!

May I ask what it is that you are doing?'

The young man paused, looked up, and replied, 'Throwing starfish into the ocean.'

'I must ask, then, why are you throwing starfish into the ocean?' asked the somewhat startled wise man.

To this, the young man replied, 'The sun is up and the tide is going out. If I don't throw them in, they'll die.'

Upon hearing this, the wise man commented, 'But, young man, do you not realize that there are miles and miles of beach and there are starfish all along every mile? You can't possibly make a difference!'

At this, the young man bent down, picked up yet another starfish, and threw it into the ocean. As it met the water, he said, 'It made a difference for that one.'

Adapted from 'The Star Thrower'
By Loren Eiseley

If you wish to follow the chapters in the order they were written, please go to Chapter 28, on page 233.

THE NAKED LEADER EXPERIENCE

deluded, or what?

'Lady Di could be bicycling nude down the street giving this book away and nobody would read it' was a genuine review of Susan Jeffers' Feel the Fear and Do It Anyway, *which became one of the most inspirational and successful books of all time.*

Sometimes the encouragement we get from other people in achieving our dreams is amazing, and sometimes, less so.

There is one question that can prevent you even starting on your dream journey.

It is the one I am asked at every seminar and event that I deliver. It is never the first question, because the person asking it wants to make sure they word it correctly. They may be worried that they are the only person who thinks it is an issue, and are waiting to see if someone else asks it first.

And no wonder it takes a while to come out, for it is the ultimate question. People will use different words, ask it with different attitudes and with varying degrees of passion. It all comes down to these six words:

When do you finally accept defeat?

A brilliant question. Here I am, going on and on about guaranteed success and removing the fear of failure (and failure itself) from our lives, spreading the message that people can be anything they want to be, yet all the time, at the back or front of people's minds, is this very question.

It basically says if you keep 'trying' or taking action and you keep being rejected, or not moving closer to your goal, maybe it was never meant to be, or maybe you do not have what it takes, so maybe you should give up.

Come on, David, we know what the question means, what's the answer?

When do you finally accept defeat?

I don't know.
I wish I did.

On New Year's Eve, a snail walked up to the bar and says, 'Can I have a pint of lager please?'

'I'm sorry, we don't serve snails in here, please go away,' replied the barman.

'A pint of lager, please,' replied the snail, very politely, 'in a straight glass.'

'Look,' the barman said, now raising his voice, 'I told you,

THE NAKED LEADER EXPERIENCE

we don't serve snails in here, now get out.'

The snail did not move, he just sat there waiting for his refreshment.

Eventually the barman could stand it no longer. 'If you don't leave now, I will throw you out of that window.'

The snail just smiled and said, 'A pint of lager, please. I want to see the New Year in, in style.'

At which point the barman picked up the snail and threw him out of the window.

A year later, to the day, on New Year's Eve, the snail returned to the bar and said, 'That hurt.'

What I do know is that most people give up, or dream smaller dreams, long before they have really gone for it – before they have really discovered what they can achieve, before they have awoken their awesome skills and potential.

Half give up at the first rejection or hurdle.

Half of the rest give up at the second or third.

Very few are left after three 'nos'.

And many of these people who have stopped will say they were deluded even to have a go – it is their excuse for bailing out.

And, of course, there will be no shortage of people around to support their view – 'give up now', 'cut your losses', 'it's not your day', etc, etc.

> *Keep the dream alive; because, you know, otherwise one day you'll go, Ooh, could I have made it? You know, and if you keep trying, at least then, when it doesn't happen, you know, you can go, At least I gave it a go, you know.*
>
> David Brent
> The Office TV Series
> Written by Ricky Gervais and Stephen Merchant

The fear of failure can kick in very early – but this feeling is nothing compared to the disappointment that comes from settling for less. It is a disappointment that will cut deep for many years to come.

And when the failure hits hardest, these are the people who moan that life has got it in for them, when in fact, by giving up too soon, they have got it in for life.

This is all a matter of balance between on the one hand giving up, and on the other, guaranteed success. At the moment giving up wins hands down. Naked Leaders aim to redress this balance – for themselves, and for everyone they know.

I urge you to make true decisions about the really important things in your life, and take action.

I urge you to follow your dreams with passion and persistence, always modifying your actions until you move closer to your dreams. And the key word in this sentence is persistence.

So many people allow the negative influences and views of others to affect them and their dreams. The simple recognition that we can be so influenced by beliefs and behaviours that do not belong to us is in itself a wonderful realization.

Indeed, when a Naked Leader turns the discussion around to help the questioner achieve their dream, it can be a breakthrough experience.

At an event for new authors, a chap told me his book had been rejected by over fifty publishers, and asked what I recommended. I asked him if he had any champagne in his fridge at home, cooled and ready to open. He said yes, they had a bottle they were keeping for a special occasion – I urged him to go home and open it that very evening, to celebrate the word 'no'.

And I urge you to celebrate the word 'no', to rejoice, and be wildly ecstatic, each and every time you hear it.

Because when you do, you will keep going, way beyond where so many others give up. And as you do so, you are learning something very valuable, namely HOW NOT to achieve something, which is very useful in helping you find HOW TO achieve it.

I started a weekly column in Computer Weekly; *after the first one was published my good friend Graham called me. Graham: 'We are running a sweepstake on how long it will be before you run out of original material.' David: 'Don't worry about that, I've got plenty of columns left in me yet.' Graham: 'It's already been won.'*

When do you finally accept defeat?
I don't know the answer to this question, but you will know how successful you are, by the number of people who reject what you are doing or thinking.

But as I don't have an answer, let's take a look at these twenty unknown, totally deluded characters:

20 Marilyn Monroe. Dropped in 1947 by 20th Century Fox after one year under contract because she was 'unattractive'.

19 Billy Joel's first album, *Cold Spring Harbour*, sold few copies. He spent the next six months playing bar piano under the pseudonym Bill Martin.

18 Jane Austen's first novel, *First Impressions*, was rejected by a publisher in 1797. Her second novel, *Northanger Abbey*, was sold in 1803 to a publisher who never published it.

17 Not only did Rock Hudson fail many screen tests before he became an actor, his screen test at 20th Century Fox was considered so bad that his audition tape was saved, and shown to others as an example of appalling acting.

16 Roger Bannister was a very deluded man – he actually believed a man could run a mile in under four minutes. Doctors even told him he would die if he attempted this feat. And guess what? Within a year of Bannister achieving his dream, over 300 other runners did exactly the same.

15 Thomas Edison 'failed' over 9,000 times before perfecting the light bulb! How many of us would have thrown in the 'proverbial' towel at twenty failures, 150 failures or at the 8,000th failure. After Edison had invented and produced the light bulb a reporter asked him how it felt to fail over 9,000 times. Edison replied, 'I was glad I found 9,000 ways not to invent the light bulb!'

14 Imagine you are in the hot seat of *Who Wants to be a Millionaire?* And you're faced with the first question, worth $100: according to the nursery rhyme, what did Little Jack Horner pull from his Christmas pie when he stuck in his thumb?

a) a plum b) a turnip c) a carrot d) a blackbird

If you want to win $100 you answer a) a plum. If you want to win fame, fortune, appearances on *Letterman*, a brand-new car and a trip to the Caribbean, you answer d) a blackbird.

That's exactly what Brian Fodera did when he panicked and froze on the spot at the very first question! After disappearing with embarrassment at being the first person in the US to fall at the first hurdle, he became a celebrity – and all based on his 'bad' experience.

From *How to Be a Celebrity* by Rosemarie Jarski

13 Elvis Presley's music teacher at L.C. Humes High School in Memphis gave him a C and told him he couldn't sing (as I mentioned before, how many of us learnt at school we weren't very good at things, and how often we are proved right?). Fortunately Elvis ignored this . . .

12 Talking of which, at my secondary school our English teacher gave a very public zero to a boy who used the Beatles song 'A Day in the Life' as his chosen piece of literature in an exam. He gained his incredibly poor mark on the grounds that it was not a 'worthy piece of literature'. Undeterred, my friend repeated his answer in his Oxford entrance exam and won a place. None of the rest of the class got to Oxford, probably because we concentrated on Chaucer . . .

11 And the Beatles themselves knew about persistence. Before they were signed by Parlaphone, they were rejected by Decca Records, Pye, Philips, Columbia and HMV. After all, guitar bands were out.

10 Samuel Johnson dropped out of Oxford in 1729 after fourteen months and never received a degree. After moving to London, virtually penniless, he wrote a book that told us what words mean! The man should have been locked up. I mean, who would ever have a need for a dictionary!

9 Lance Armstrong. Lance was diagnosed with testicula cancer. How did he react? As he went through years of pain, he fought it with everything he had. And when he recovered he went on to win the *Tour De France* for a fourth time and set out on a mission to give hope to all those suffering from this 'taboo of cancers'. As he says, 'When I heard the words, "You have cancer", I thought, *pain, temporary; quitting lasts forever*'.

8 The Bee. I know it's not a person; however this insect is totally deluded, for bees actually believe they can fly! Bumble bees, according to the known laws of aerodynamics, should not be able to fly. Fortunately, bumble bees don't read much about aerodynamics, so they don't realize they are doing something they are not supposed to be able to do.

7 James Redfield's *The Celestine Prophecy* was widely rejected, but just before delusion kicked in, he self-published it. Just as well he did, for it has become one of the biggest selling mind-body-spirit books in the history of publishing, ten million (plus) copies later.

6 Cameron Mackintosh decided to produce a musical about felines at a venue (the New London) that had never had a hit. Most people thought him mad, and certainly deluded. Yet *Cats* became one of the longest-running musicals ever. A few years later, clearly not having learned his lesson, he produced another show, wait for it, set in pre-revolutionary France, featuring poverty, death and despair. How entertaining is that? It opened to very small audiences at the Barbican in London and almost every critic hated it.

Cameron would surely finally accept defeat, wouldn't he?

I'm afraid not. *Les Misérables* is now the most successful musical in the world.

5 Anthony Robbins was thrown out of his home at age seventeen and spent many years living in a tiny one-room apartment. One day, when he did not have enough money to pay for the electricity and it was turned off, he faced up to his choice. Was he going to live this life (this 'reality') or was he going to make a different decision?

He is now the single most successful motivational speaker in the world, and he certainly no longer lives in a one-room apartment!

4 Winston Churchill was branded a 'warmonger' by most of his British parliamentary colleagues, the media and, indeed, many of the population of the United Kingdom. I mean, the very idea that this nice guy Adolf was going to hurt anyone, come on . . .

3 After years of rejection, an American novelist started a story about a teenager named Carietta White. Disgusted with what he had written, he screwed up the pages and threw them in the rubbish bin. His wife pulled those pages out of the bin, read them, and then convinced her husband to complete the story – which became the huge bestseller *Carrie*. Stephen King is now one of the most successful authors of all time.

2 Nelson Mandela was imprisoned on Robben Island for twenty-seven years as punishment for his efforts opposing apartheid. That's twenty-seven years. Yet he never gave up his beliefs about what was right, he never gave up his dream, and he never stopped believing that his work, or that of his supporters, would prevail.

1 You. Please, whatever you are doing right now, revisit what you most dream, desire and deserve. Perhaps it is new; perhaps it is an old wish, dusted off anew. It may be personal; it may be reconnecting with your partner or your children. It may be forgiving someone in your family, after many years. It may be to do with your work or career.

Whatever it is – please go for it, and be the very best that you already are.

And as you do, always remember, it will be those people who tell you that you are deluded, that will be the first to tell you, when you achieve your dream, 'I always knew you would be successful.'

And in answer to that question, 'When do you finally accept defeat?' I think I've worked it out: when people ask this question, it often says a lot about their own minds, beliefs and fears. Deep-down, they want reassurance, they seek permission, and they crave to reawaken an inner calling.

So, the 'answer' I now give: Whenever you so choose.

One thing's for sure, the twenty examples above are not unique, there are thousands if not millions of people who keep going, every single day, in all walks of life, and against all odds.

And so, next time you come up against a brick wall, will you bang your head against it, or kick it down?

Deluded, or what?

I choose the 'What' every time.

'We never know how high we are till we are called to rise'
Emily Dickinson

So, are you going to decide to be the very best that you already are?

Or are you still waiting around? Always remember, ships look great in port, but it's not what they're built for.

I am often asked about people who come from poor backgrounds, and who are 'disadvantaged'. What chances of success do they have?

Actually, a greater chance than people from so-called 'comfortable' backgrounds. Perhaps it is through belief or determination or thanks to a little help. With a little encouragement, anything is possible . . .

This is a true story, with names changed:

Sarah's Story

'I was a baby when Dad left, but Mum always had boyfriends. They all hit or verbally abused me. I didn't tell anyone, I didn't understand what was wrong. I just wanted my mum to love me.

'I felt so worthless I started self-harming at nine. I cut myself where no-one would see. I was also bullied at school. Being chubby and wearing glasses made me a target for other kids. Even moving to another school didn't help.

'Things changed a bit when I was fifteen. I joined a drama club and met people who liked me. But Mum didn't like them and after a huge row she banned me from seeing

them. It was the final straw. I packed some clothes and left.

'I went to Social Services, but I wasn't classified as "at immediate risk" so they couldn't help. The hostels wouldn't take me as I was under sixteen and the police said they'd take me home! I had no choice, I went home but things were bad, so I left with nowhere to go, no money, no clothes – nothing.

'I wasn't on the streets long when I found the Children's Society Safe in the City project. It helps children who run away.

'I met the project workers. They brought me clean clothes, soap, toothpaste and food. I was really grateful. More important they listened to and believed me, it made such a difference.

'They advised on what services I could get, came along to Social Services meetings and fought my corner – something no-one had done before.

'I'm twenty now with my own flat. And I'm off to university. The Children's Society helped me move my life forward. I don't know where I would be without them.'

The Children's Society works directly in ninety places in England, with 36,000 children and teenagers living through problems no young person should face. By campaigning, fundraising and giving these children a voice, the society helps them to move their lives forward. (*www.childrenssociety.org.uk*)

If you wish to follow the chapters in the order they were written, please go to Chapter 8, on page 73.

loyalty – release the leaders within

'The next big thing is people. The problem is people are waiting for the next big thing.'
Paul Stephenson, EGOstream

I made a mistake in Book One, and I would now like to correct it.

I said that I believed that people are an organization's number-one asset. I was wrong: people are an organization's *only* asset. Indeed, people are an organization.

And they are your route to success.

Win over the loyalty of your people, and everything else will look after itself. Your success will be automatic.

Let's look at the evidence: over the last twenty years, we've 'done' technology, customer relationships, processes, initiatives, change and, of course, quality. And here we are, not a great deal further forward, still looking for the way to overcome all of the challenges we face.

And all the time, the choices we have, the decisions we need to make and the actions we must take all lie within.

Everything we need to be anything we want, lies waiting and within us, and our organization. And they have been there all along, throughout the last twenty-year rollercoaster ride.

- **The first big 'up' – the Eighties – all going well – how much money can we make?**

- **Early Nineties – massive drop – a few fall out (those at the bottom, of course).**

- **Mid-Nineties – time for some expensive change initiatives. Quick, outsource the children, downsize your spouse and re-engineer the cat.**

- **Early twenty-first century – another drop into global recession.**

- **Now – final stop at base . . . less people on board, who must all work harder and give so much more . . .**

The ride has come to the end, what happens next is up to you. You can give up, go round the same circuit again, with the same results.

Or you can change the ride.

Your choice.

And to help you make your decision, read the most important paragraph you will ever read about inspiring human beings:

People will only ever do something to the best of their ability for one reason, and one reason alone. Because they want to.

We can pay them large salaries, we can punish them with warnings, or we can patronize them with quality initiatives. It makes no difference.

From the moment you took your first breath on this earth to the moment you take your last, you will only ever do something – anything – to the very best of your ability, using your amazing strengths, gifts and energy to the full, if, and only if, you choose to.

If there is anyone inside your organization or project or team that is not giving their very best, it is their choice, and their decision. No-one else's.

As managers we 'try' to change that, but as leaders we know we cannot change another human being. True change must come from within, not without.

The decision to change, to give more, and to be more, must be made by the person, the teams, the communities, themselves.

And when that happens . . . success happens.

Yet, while we cannot actually change another person, there are some very powerful actions we can take to encourage them to make that change, to inspire people, and to ensure they make choices that take projects, teams and organizations forward.

The Top Twenty Ways to Motivate People:

20 Paint a clear, concise and compelling vision

•   **That appeals to people's hearts AND minds.**

- **Involve as many people as you can in its painting.**

- **Share the vision with your people – if anything is not clear, say so, and ask for ideas, ask for help.**

- **Keep focusing on where you want to go, not what you want to avoid.**

19 Put the past behind you

Apologize for the past if you feel genuinely sorry for the way you or your company handled or created problems. Emphasize the now and the future.

18 Be open and visible

- **Be present – face to face, as often as possible.**

- **Allocate enough time to listen to people – and *do* listen.**

- **Get to know names and something about the private world of as many people as possible. The personal touch matters.**

- **Avoid the 'meet the manager' style buffet lunches where everyone stands around awkwardly and talks to you as if you are 'special', i.e. not one of 'them'. These situations create barriers.**

17 Separate 'respect' from 'like'

You have to earn people's respect; you do not need people to 'like' you. Focus on building and earning respect at work, by being true to what you say and do.

16 **Accept all mistakes as your own, and take the praise for nothing**

- Everything is your fault.

- Even when you are on holiday (you'll be blamed behind your back anyway, may as well make it official!).

- When you praise someone, be specific on why they are being praised (or it sounds false).

- Praise openly and honestly. When things go wrong, have open words, in private, and ensure that they stay private.

15 **Put clear values in place**

Values are the fastest way to transform 'culture', because they put in place a set of principles and behaviours for people to live and work by – and your people define your culture. Make sure you involve others in deciding the values (you will find an amazing degree of agreement).

Don't overanalyse your values, they will die (e.g. 'fun' or 'teamwork' may be values and need to be understood, but not endlessly debated).

Finally, make sure that you and your immediate leadership team live by them, always.

14 **Trust your people 100 per cent**

- It's up to you to earn their trust, based on who you are, what you do and what you say, in that order of impact.

- It's up to your team to lose your trust – and when they

start to do so, tell them in private how they can win it back.

13 When communicating – remember who you are

As manager or leader, you have power over others. So, when you communicate, take actions that reduce your physical power, or people may be fearful of you and not 'get' your messages. When you communicate in the department, sit down so you are at the same level, and when speaking, ask more questions than you make statements.

12 Hold open forums (or, as someone once insisted, 'fora!')

- **Twice a month, once in the morning and once in the late afternoon.**

- **Plant questions at the first one or two – tricky questions that you will answer.**

- **Speak for five minutes only, keep the rest for questions.**

- **Make them voluntary – and keep holding them if no-one turns up – just eat the sandwiches yourself!**

11 Recruit people with crazy and fresh ideas

We need people who think differently from ourselves, and who do not so much think outside the box, as leave the box behind. They can be attracted internally or externally, however make sure that you or your leadership team do not interview them – or you will recruit more of the same types of people!

10 **Put fun back into work**

This genuine internal advertisement attracted three responses from a company with 4,000 people.

Department	Information Systems
Team	Applications Development
Job Title	Senior Analyst
Job Grade	6 (Pending Appeal)
Hours	Standard with Overtime
Description of Role	(Too Long and Boring to Reprint Here)
To Apply	Phone HR Department – Int: 2477

The next internal advertisement for the same job in the same team attracted ninety-two responses.

IF YOU WANT A QUIET LIFE . . . JOIN A MONASTERY

IF YOU WANT SOME FUN, JOIN US

PHONE MIKE – INT: 2477

9 **Give people standards to live up to . . .**

- **Have an Internet access policy. However, the stricter the rules, the more people will break them.**

- **Positively encourage people to leave work early and work odd hours by doing the same yourself.**

8 Make sure you have fast, focused and flexible structures

Make it circular with you in the centre, or if HR won't allow that make it upside down, with you at the bottom and your customer-facing people at the top. Ideally don't have a structure, rather have 'domains' of responsibility, with each domain having an owner. People can move in and out of domains according to work and project demand. That way you get over the 'subordinates = power' syndrome.

7 Measure morale

Avoid loads of questions, it's how people feel right now that matters. Ask them how they rank their personal morale – zero to ten – zero very unhappy, ten deliriously happy.

If they won't do it openly by sharing it out loud, do it secretly by paper – then take an average and share that figure. Vote yourself and tell your team your vote and why.

If the figures are high ask what is going well (and do more of the same) and if the figures are low, ask what needs to change.

6 Catch people doing things right

When you hear about someone doing well, or when a project is delivered, go and thank the person personally. If they are several levels 'below' you (or 'above' you in an upside-down structure!) it is even more powerful. Never congratulate an individual by email, and never say what one manager did to his project team (of six) on completion of a successful project (verbatim – I was there): 'Well done, everyone. Sorry, I've only been here six months so I don't know all of your names – I know yours, Mike, well done, and yours, Clare, no, sorry Cathy, well done. (Awkward pause.) Anyway, personally I'm amazed that it went so well. Incredible. Well done again.' (Disappears into office.)

5 **Put in place a specialist ladder**

- **It can be a disaster when technical people are promoted to manage others just to reward them with a decent grade. Often, these people do not want to manage people, they want to manage 'things'.**

- **Have a separate structure for this category, if you have to, that pays them without giving them people leadership that they may not want.**

4 **Find out why people stay, or enjoy working with your company.**

Ask people why they work for you. I am not suggesting you rush up to someone you haven't spoken to for a month and shout, 'Why do you work here?' I am suggesting that over a period of time you find out the main reasons people enjoy working with you, in the course of normal conversation. Note how few say 'money'. Also, ask them for one idea that they have – just the one – that they would do if they were you. (And if you put this into action, make sure you credit the idea properly.)

3 **Set them free**

* Make sure everyone is valued and respected.

* Ensure people know what decisions they can and cannot make, and set them free within those guidelines. Trust them with certain boundaries and they will deliver.

* Projects are over-managed – set the outcome, budget and time scale, then put in place a team and let them get on with it.

2 **Self-determined pay**

How far dare you go . . . ?

Step One (A Given)

* Avoid the stress of performance assessment by putting in 360-degree appraisals (everyone is assessed from above, below and from their peers).

Step Two (Brave)

* Avoid the greater stress of pay time by asking people to self-assess what they earn – when you get the culture right you will find people will mark themselves down, and include yourself in this.

Step Three (You Hero)

* If you feel really brave, let your people decide how much you should receive. Get them together and tell them the

'pot' is 100 per cent. Invite them to split it openly with full agreement. If they cannot, ask them privately to indicate what they feel they each personally deserve, but make it clear you have the final say.

* I know several teams that decide their own pay every year.

① Put in place a contract:

You promise to:

* Guarantee their skill development.

* Support them in this development.

* Involve them in real decision making.

* Open up real opportunities.

And in return, your people promise to:

* Develop and apply the skills you need.

* Take collective responsibility.

* Behave consistent with agreed values.

* Be team players with a commitment to each other.

The speech that rekindled loyalty and arguably won the US Civil War . . .

Was not the Gettysburg Address, it was the speech that Colonel Chamberlain gave to a large group of deserters that had been given to him the day before the biggest battle of the entire war.

And he desperately needed them to join his Northern Maine regiment for the upcoming battle.

Impeccably researched, and based on *The Killer Angels* by Michael Shaara, the film *Gettysburg* is the definitive account of the Battle of Gettysburg, a battle that saw more men killed in three days than died in the entire Vietnam War.

And in that battle, many historians agree that Colonel Chamberlain's holding of Little Round Top won the day, and was the turning point in the whole war, in favour of the North.

As you read his speech, made entirely off the cuff, note his skills at using the word 'we', his constant linking of the overall aim of the war with the present choice the men face, and, most of all, his repeated use of three points together, one of the most powerful techniques in presentations. I have underlined the threes, because of their power.

Colonel Chamberlain approached all of the deserters just after they arrived, and spoke to them together, as a group. What followed is quite simply the most powerful, passionate and persuasive speech I have ever seen re-enacted on film:

I've been ordered to take you men with me, I'm told that if you [laughs quietly] don't come I can shoot you. Well, you know I won't do that. Maybe somebody else will, but I won't, so that's that.

Here's the situation, the whole Reb army is up that road aways waiting for us, so this is no time for an argument like this, I tell you. We could surely use you fellahs, we're now well below half strength.

THE NAKED LEADER EXPERIENCE

Whether you fight or not, that's up to you, whether you come along is is . . . well, you're coming.

You know who we are and what we are doing here, but if you are going to fight alongside us there are a few things I want you to know.

This regiment was formed last summer, in Maine.

There were a thousand of us then, there are less than three hundred of us now.

All of us volunteered to fight for the Union, just as you have.

Some came mainly because we were bored at home, thought this looked like it might be fun.

Some came because we were ashamed not to.

Many of us came because it was the right thing to do.

And all of us have seen men die.

This is a different kind of army.

If you look back through history you will see men fighting for pay, for women, for some other kind of loot.

They fight for land, power, because a king leads them, or just because they like killing.

But we are here for something new, this has not happened much, in the history of the world.

We are an army out to set other men free.

America should be free ground, all of it, not divided by a line between slave states and free – all the way from here to the Pacific Ocean.

No man has to bow. No man born to royalty.

Here we judge you by what you do, not by who your father was.

Here you can be something.

Here is the place to build a home.

But it's not the land, there's always more land.

It's the idea that we all have value – you and me.

What we are fighting for, in the end, we're fighting for each other.

Sorry, I didn't mean to preach.

You go ahead and you talk for a while.

If you choose to join us and you want your muskets back you can have them – nothing more will be said by anyone anywhere.

If you choose not to join us well then you can come along under guard and when this is all over I will do what I can to ensure you get a fair trial, but for now we're moving out.

Gentlemen, I think if we lose this fight we lose the war, so if you choose to join us I will be personally very grateful.

From *Gettysburg* (Jeff Daniels as Colonel Chamberlain) Written and directed by Ronald F. Maxwell

114 out of 120 deserters joined with the regiment immediately, with another four joining later.

If you wish to follow the chapters in the order they were written, please go to Chapter 39, on page 331.

the mind game

While the power of the mind has been accepted, and indeed integrated, into most sports, it has yet to really take off in football. And no wonder – after all, what role has our thinking and beliefs in such a man's game, where physical aggression, skill and fitness are everything?

Or are they?

The first football team I worked with, over five years ago, was very sceptical. So I stood in front of them, between two flip-charts, and asked what they had to do to win a match. They yawned, made various remarks I can't repeat here, and laughed. After a few moments one of them shouted, 'Score more goals than we let in.' I wrote it down on the chart next to me. Another yelled, 'Pass the ball' – to great mocking from his teammates. I wrote this down as well.

Then, silence.

After a while another player (now a household name) said, with a disparaging voice, 'Speak to each other.' I raced across the room, wrote this down on another chart, and ran back again. I repeated this for the next ten minutes as people started to speak openly, only now using words like *belief*, *passion* and *confidence*.

At the end, one flip-chart (the fitness and technical skills) had two contributions, the other flip-chart (the belief and mental skills) over fifty. Jaws on the floor, we started working together.

And that's it. The aim of football is to score more goals than you let in. It really is the simplest game in the world, and there are just three factors that decide how a team, and the players in that team, perform: fitness, technical skills and mental skills (the Mind Game).

Of course, the Mind Game can be powerfully applied to many different sports.

Now, given that the first two are understood, what are the key parts of the Mind Game that make a difference?

- **Focus – the ability to concentrate in the moment. Concentrate on just one thing at a time and trust that everything else will happen automatically. See yourself playing well, in your mind, see yourself passing the ball and scoring – see it over and over. As we've explored already, your imagination is very powerful and cannot tell the difference between 'reality' and anything you imagine with emotional intensity.**

- **Emotional Balance – how you feel throughout the game, your 'state'. Put yourself in a peak state at the start of the game, using the team huddle as your cue – and stay in this state until the final whistle.**

- **Want – your determination to win. The players and team that WANT to win most, will win, it's as simple as that.**

And as a team:

- **If you feel invincible as a team – play as if you are invincible.**

- **If you do not feel invincible as a team – play as if you are invincible.**

When we apply all of these principles in any sport we enter an area called 'the Zone'. In the Zone outstanding play is automatic.

And that is the Mind Game.

To play it you do not need a psychologist, a magician or a spoon bender (although that is what you will be called). The only magic is in the results.

Woking FC . . .

Picture the scene – the final match on the final day of the 2002–2003 season. The team have to win to avoid relegation. I had been working with them for several weeks, and had gained their trust. Now, I had to deliver something very special.

I watched Kenneth Branagh's speech in Henry V *for inspiration – and this is an extract of what I read.*

If these words made any difference, it is down to the players, Woking's managers Glenn Cockerill and Matt Crossley, and not to me . . .

And so it is all down to the last ninety minutes of the season, all down to the here and now, all down to you.

*. . . It really doesn't matter how you as an individual believe we got into this position – you only have to read five different papers to get five different reasons – the changes in managers, the pitch, luck . . . it really doesn't matter what has happened before, all that matters now, **all** that matters, is that you win today . . .*

*. . . I want to talk just for a few seconds about the Zone, I've touched on the Zone before – it is the most powerful area available to you today, right now, if you so choose. It is entirely your choice. Sometimes when you approach a big game fear and nerves can kick in – long before match day. This week has been the longest week of my life, so I would imagine for all of you it's lasted about a year. Basically, the Zone is the complete opposite of fear – it is the place where you know, you **absolutely know**, that every pass you make will be on target, when you shoot at goal it will be on target – the Zone is the place where you stop playing football and you start **being** a footballer – you just are a footballer – you don't have to think about what you are doing because it happens, naturally . . .*

(I then talked about Association, as in Chapter 30, on page 255.)

. . . You may not believe this, but I believe a lot of players would love to be in your shoes today, because you are about to play a match with real meaning. Not one of these boring end-of-season mid-table matches.

You are the chosen few.

You are the chosen few that are going out here, together, on Saturday 26th April.

You will remember this afternoon for the rest of your lives. You will remember it whatever the result, every single day, so you may as well win it and remember it well.

In years to come you will put your children, your grand-children, on your knee, and say to them, 'I was there – I was there, at Kingfield, on Saturday 26th April, when all of the hard work, belief and commitment finally came together, I was part of that team.'

Gentlemen, it has been a real privilege to work with you, a real honour, and if you would be ever so good as to go out today and win, I know a whole town who will be personally very grateful.

Thank you.

Dedicated with thanks to everyone at Woking Football Club. They responded on the day by winning 3–0, and avoided relegation.

If you wish to follow the chapters in the order they were written, please go to Chapter 32, on page 279.

choice 22

Note for people reading this book from front to back. This was the last chapter I wrote. It covers Reclaim, Reignite and Reinvent, and is positioned here because this is number 22. Why 22, and not at the end? All will be revealed.

The film *Forrest Gump* is best known for its quote about chocolates: 'Life is like a box of chocolates, you never know what you're gonna get.'

I've never really understood this famous line, because with a box of chocolates you always get a guide, a picture showing what each chocolate is, so that the eater can make an informed choice.

So, if life was really like a box of chocolates, we'd all get guides on the day we were born.

But, of course, it isn't, so we make up our own rules as we go along.

Our 'answers'.

Helped by many others, of course: parents, school, anyone and everyone we meet. Plus all those proverbs that were quoted to us, and caused us such confusion:

- **Should we look before we leap, or is he who hesitates lost?**

- **Do many hands make light work, or too many cooks spoil the broth?**

- **Is out of sight out of mind, or does absence make the heart grow fonder?**

Based on what we choose to believe, we build up more and more answers to help us get through life. We acquire knowledge, full of facts and the way things really are, we live through experiences, and we learn how life really is, and we open up our imaginations, to the way that life could be – in our dreams, in books and at the cinema.

We are all walking geniuses.

And then a few years ago I made a discovery that changed my life for ever. I suppose I should have spotted it many years previously. I was obviously a bit slow.

Other people had a different answer sheet to me.

Indeed, everyone had a different answer sheet to each other.

And what's more, as they were 'handed' their answers, they were already marked and assessed by their teachers, and bizarrely although everyone had different answers to the same questions, everyone was scored with full marks.

And yet, if our answers are different, how can that be?

Because you and I are both right, every time. You live your life by your answers; I live mine, by mine.

In my research for the *Naked Leader* books, I attended many leadership events and seminars. Many of them would begin with the facilitator saying: 'Now, by the end of this course, if I have done my job properly, you will have more questions than answers.'

And I always felt a bit cheated by that. Not just because I was doing 'research' and the aim of 'research' is to find answers, but because I could have done with some clear, concise and compelling ways to navigate this thing called life.

And so here you are, indeed, here we are. No matter how you have reached this chapter, whether you have followed a journey (in which case this is your 'final' chapter), decided to read the book from start to finish (in which case you are halfway through) or have just randomly opened this page, we have, right now, reached exactly the same point, and we have reached it together.

Searching for the answers and, failing that, searching for the questions.

And what have we in front of us now?

Choices.

There is a famous book, *I Ching*. That book is known as the book of changes.

This book is the book of choices.

A native American grandfather was talking to his grandson about how he felt. He said, 'I feel as if I have two wolves fighting in my heart. One wolf is the vengeful, angry, violent one. The other wolf is the loving, compassionate one.' The grandson asked him, 'Which wolf will win the

fight in your heart? The grandfather answered, 'The one I feed.'
Native American story

There are many choices in this book, and in our lives. Ideas, actions, knowledge, information ... They are thrown out like confetti, and yet what will work for one person, one team or one organization, may not work for another.

So, please, catch some of these ideas and if you feel they are appropriate for you, put them into action.

Let others wait.

And I will take that one stage further. Because I believe that it is through the choices that are before us, the true decisions that we then make and how much we really, really want to achieve our dreams, that we find the answers.

Many, many answers spring from those choices and decisions that are best for you, your family, your team and your organization.

And by 'best' I mean choices that take you closer to your dreams, in the shortest possible time.

Your personal answers may be out there in the ether, they may be in your imagination right now, or you may be awaiting their arrival.

OK, what about business and personal development books? They must be full of answers.

Recently a reviewer for *UK Director* magazine said that 'all those ten-steps-to-heaven books' ought to be chased off the management shelves.

No – the more books and different types of books we have available to us, the more likely we are to find our answers. Indeed, one of the reasons for political extremism such as fascism is that people are encouraged to only read one book, or books giving the same message.

I say this: read lots of different books, listen to many points of view, reflect on the conflicting views, and then decide what works for you, in your life, and what will not.

So, if you don't agree with something I have written in this book, then look at what I have suggested, and do the complete opposite.

And if you don't agree with anything in this book, then please have another look – because throughout this book I have deliberately put in 'answers' and choices that conflict with each other, to widen your options.

Oh, for the world of certainty, give me mathematics anytime, I can almost hear you say.

Well, let's not forget that mathematics has its root in the occult, and many people lost their lives for openly practising it.

I believe that true enlightenment comes with being aware of the choices we have before us, no matter what our age, our background or our present circumstances.

And respecting that others may have made different choices, different beliefs and different answers is the key.

I think if we all did that the world would be a more enjoyable place to live, for everyone.

And it can be, if we so choose.

Ultimately, the answers that we carry around with us become our truth, and that becomes our life, and so often we then try to persuade others that something about our life is right and theirs is wrong.

I met a woman in a bookshop the other day. She and I were chatting, and she asked about *The Naked Leader*.

I said that my aim was to strip away all of the mystery, the hype and jargon around success, leadership and life.

To which she asked: 'And what does that leave you with?'

Silence.

And then she walked out – not with a smile, not with a look that said 'ah-ha – got you', but with a very friendly, warm and caring look. I would like to thank that person.

'What does that leave you with?'

You.

It leaves you with you.

Wonderful, living, breathing, unique, talented, gifted, humble, caring, awesome, magnificent.

You.

Imagine if you simply could not fail: who would you be?

You would be you.

No matter which books you have believed, and which you have rejected.

No matter where you are right now, or where you have come from.

No matter where you are travelling to, and how you will get there.

There is only one, common denominator.

You.

And it suddenly rushed over me.

One of the reasons we are looking for answers is because we don't want to face up to all those choices, we want someone else to supply us with the answers. And yet, all of our choices, all of our own answers, lie within us.

The other person I am so grateful to works in HMV in Oxford Street in London.

When I pulled this book together, I did not know where it was going to end. I wanted it to be significant to the messages within the book, and I wanted it to be different to book one, which ended on 42 in homage to Douglas Adams.

I was in HMV, browsing. I noticed a book section that I had not previously seen, and decided to buy two books, and took them to the counter.

'You know you can get three books for the price of two?' the young chap serving me said.

I hadn't spotted the huge yellow stickers on all of the books!

I was about the leave the queue and go to select a third book, when I paused, and asked him, 'Would you mind doing me a favour? Would you go and select a book for me please?'

After some gentle persuasion, he did so (I convinced him that it really did not matter, because any book would be a bonus).

He walked over to the books and without a moment's hesitation selected *Catch 22* by Joseph Heller.

And as he handed it to me he said, 'I think this book is perfect for you.'

And it was.

Catch 22 – what an amazing book, a bestseller by a brilliant author, a classic by any definition.

I sat down on a bench in Oxford Street, and immersed myself in the book, one I had read many years before.

The sounds of traffic and the people all disappeared as I sat for three hours reading about the imaginary island of Pianosa during the Second World War. The novel centres on Captain Yossarian and his attempts to survive as part of a bomber squadron long enough to get home. Yossarian discovers the ultimate 'catch':

> *[A man] would be crazy to fly more missions and sane if he didn't, but he was sane, he had to fly them. If he flew then he was crazy and didn't have to; but if he didn't, he was sane, and had to.*

And the book became such a cult hit that the term 'catch-22' has become a part of our language, defined in the *Oxford Dictionary* as:

> *A situation or predicament from which it is impossible to extricate yourself, because of built-in illogical rules and regulations.*

Basically this means that in many areas of our lives, we have no choice. Whatever we do, we cannot move forward, we will always return to our starting point, so there is no point in doing something in the first place. We cannot win.

There are no real choices open to us, especially for the big decisions in our lives.

And so, in homage to Joseph Heller, I decided to end this book on 22.

However, I have a different view from Joseph – a difference that is in these three ideas:

Firstly, it is in those precise situations that Joseph describes, where we feel we have no choice whatsoever, that we are on the verge of making the biggest decisions in our lives. When we feel we have no choice, it is the choice we discover that can be the breakthrough.

In short, when it can't be done, do it. Because if you don't do it, it doesn't exist.

You invented it.

A new idea cannot be judged or measured or even described. It first needs to exist.

To be made.

Secondly, although catch-22 describes a situation in which we cannot win, I believe that this approach, along with the classic Murphy's Law (if it can go wrong it will go wrong), provides the perfect excuse for us not to see the different choices to negativity.

We can reverse this. In every situation we believe we do not have a choice, we decide that we do, and start looking for them. Because of the way we work as human beings (our subconscious will always provide the answer for whatever we ask it) we will find them.

We always have choices, although they may not be clear at first.

And my third and final inspiration from *Catch-22* comes down to this simple deduction: either you believe you have choices in your life or you do not.

Many people believe we have choices in any and every situation in our lives, while others believe we do not have choices in our lives.

Who is right?

Ah, now you are expecting me to say: they both are.

Well, on this occasion, may I have your permission to differ from myself?

Because I believe that whether we have choices in our lives is a matter of opinion, it is a matter of belief, it is a matter of choice.

If you believe you have a choice, then you have a choice.

And if you do not believe you have a choice, then you have a choice.

Because by believing what you believe, you are making a choice in itself.

You are making the very thing that you believe you do not have.

Therefore you must have it.

Therefore you have choice.

Welcome to the antithesis of catch-22, the central message of catch-22 is: sometimes we have no choice. Whatever we do, we will always return to our starting point, so there is no point in doing something in the first place. We cannot win.

I say this: always, we have choice. Whatever we do, we will always move somewhere, so there is every point in doing something in the first place. We cannot lose.

And this is especially true for the big decisions in our lives, when we feel we have no choices. It is opening up our minds, and our hearts, to the fact that we have choices, always, that will shape our lives into a destiny.

Your Future – your Choice, and no-one else's.

We may not always be able to control events, but we can always choose how we react to those events – what meaning we give to each and every event that ever happens to us.

And that is a powerful choice to make, the choice of attitude.

And when we do that, we take 'reality' by surprise.

And, taking it one stage further, when we choose how we react to events, we find that events begin to unfold as if we are ourselves shaping them – we find resources and help when we most need it, we find life, wonderful life, seems to help us achieve our dreams.

And as you read this, and you think about choices, you may find yourself making some decisions, some true decisions:

THE NAKED LEADER EXPERIENCE

- **To come out of the shadows.**

- **To lay down the burdens you have been carrying, and come home.**

- **To be the very best that you already are.**

Living a life – fulfilling our dreams, and knowing when it is our time to leave this earth that we have no regrets – comes down to one thing: knowing you are already good enough, the question is how good you want to be.

Because you already have everything you need, to be anything you want.

So, you can stop searching for the magic, the miracle, and the magnificent in life: you've found it. You are it. And now, right now, you decide:

'Life's a bitch and then you die.'
Or
'Life's a wonder, and now you live.'

Trials never end, of course. Unhappiness and misfortune are bound to occur as long as people live, but there is a feeling now, that was not here before, and is not just on the surface of things, but penetrates all the way through: We've won it. It's going to get better now. You can sort of tell these things.

Zen and The Art of Motorcycle Maintenance
Robert M. Pirsig

impress your boss!

No matter how much we know about building rapport with our colleagues and acquaintances, all of the rules seem to leap out of the window when it comes to our bosses.

The irony is, of course, that it is with him/her that it is most important that conversations and meetings go well. Because of this importance we often freeze, get tongue-tied or, worse still, simply ramble on incoherently!

I was once about to meet a very, very well-known business leader and entrepreneur. I wanted to make the right first impression, and as I waited in his office I asked his assistant how he liked to be greeted.

She said: 'Oh, he is always giving an opinion on something in the news, so if you just listen and say something like "indeed" you can't go wrong.'

And then the guy rushed in, and said, 'Hello, David, I've been really looking forward to meeting you.'

I froze, that was the last thing I expected him to say!

And almost subconsciously I blurted out: 'Indeed.'

The lessons we learn!

Here are three chance opportunities that will happen to you often in your career, with different people, and how to turn them to your advantage:

1 The 60-second encounter, e.g. a lift journey

How to make a good first impression even if you have previously only had limited contact.

Your Aim: To give an immediate great impression.

The Usual Pitfall: Most people panic in short time periods, say far too much and regret it afterwards.

How to Achieve your Aim: Look at him/her straight in the eyes, smile warmly (and genuinely), hold out your hand to shake theirs and say, 'Hi, my name is xxxx, I work in your team helping customers to xxxx.'

Of all the options you have in such a short space of time, customers are the ace-card – you cannot go wrong mentioning them.

Add a specific about what you do – a real example – to show how you help customers.

Eye contact is critical.

The phrase 'your team' lets the person know you work for them, without appearing to be too crawling. This also lets them know they are the boss (playing to their ego).

When you have said your piece be quiet – they will fill the gap – the 60 seconds will then come to an end – smile a warm goodbye (only shake their hand again if they offer it).

You will be remembered.

2 The 60-minute dialogue, e.g. a lunch (how to impress him/her if you've never really entered into a meaningful dialogue before)

Your Aim: To make the lunch memorable, for all the right reasons!

Do	Don't
Show enthusiasm at having the chance to talk.	Expect the worst, or bad news, be confident and assertive.
If your boss drinks a glass of wine, have one, but nurse it.	Drink alcohol if he or she doesn't.
Have a friendly conversation.	Hijack the lunch onto your own agenda.
If you are with the opposite sex, remember, you are after mutual respect, not friendship or more.	Allow the matter to be discussed to be rushed through. Your opinion is valuable.

The Usual Pitfall: Most people talk more than they listen, and even then, they do not really listen.
With thanks to *New Woman* magazine

3 The 6-hour endurance, e.g. a train/plane journey (how to really work on strengthening your bond with your boss without getting on his/her nerves)

The biggest challenge!

Your Aim: To ensure you and your boss feel comfortable in each other's company.

The Usual Pitfall: Most people will waffle (in particular, feeling the need to fill gaps) and laugh too loudly at jokes or attempted jokes.

How to Achieve your Aim: This is a long haul – so allow plenty of natural silences, allow your boss to dictate the overall topics of conversation and let them flow naturally. Let him/her speak for two thirds of the conversation. Keep the conversation light unless they take it deeper. During long breaks read paperwork from the office, or simply relax. (Avoid falling asleep as it can be embarrassing if you rest your head on their shoulder, or if you wake up with saliva dripping from your mouth!)

Be genuine in your conversation and in your interest in your boss – they are human just like you, and will remember you well for feeling at ease. The safest area of conversation is their family, in particular their children, grandchildren, etc, and second safest is their background.

They will tell you their life story given the chance. And do ask questions and show an interest no matter how boring this may be. Comment on areas and experiences you have in common.

And when they attempt a funny comment or joke, look at them and simply smile – there is no need to silence the whole carriage with hysterical laughter.

Rule of thumb: if you feel comfortable during the journey, they will be feeling the same.

* * *

THE NAKED LEADER EXPERIENCE

Finally, for all three situations, if you cannot think of anything to say, simply repeat back what they have said to you – in your own words. Do it naturally, and you will be amazed at the power. Because what you are saying is, 'Hey, you – I've been listening to every single word you have told me, and that means I think you are important.'

Being 'important' is a very high priority for us all. And by repeating their words back in your own style and manner you are also checking for understanding, and buying valuable time to relax, and think about what to say next.

Delia Hyde, CEO of Rain Communications, shares this wonderful story of how to really impress a client!

I had lunch with a very important new client.

I ordered a main course and my guest asked for a side salad. I assumed she was on a diet.

When the food arrived, I tucked in with great enthusiasm. I asked my guest if she would like a couple of prawns from my plate, as the portion was huge. I also chucked her over a few chips.

It was only when I'd left the restaurant that the penny dropped – my main course was for two to share! My client had ordered the side salad to go with the main course. I recalled in horror how the waitress had placed the food in the middle of the table and how, thinking it a bit odd, I had simply grabbed the plate and tucked in.

I wondered what the two empty plates were for.

I'd only eaten my client's lunch!

I rang her and apologized profusely – she admitted she'd been puzzled – in between bursts of laughter. That day we made a connection and, five years later, we do great work together.

Whatever we do in life, we must remember it's the 'feeling' that provides a long-lasting, powerful connection. And that connection brings the all-important relationships to life.

www.raincommunications.co.uk

If you wish to follow the chapters in the order they were written, please go to Chapter 41, on page 345.

the face is familiar

Touch your finger on your forehead and say, 'This is the most powerful computer on the planet, it records every-thing that ever happens to me, from the moment I was born to the moment I die.'

How much of our brain do we actually use, as average human beings, on a daily basis? A few years ago, scientists, academics and experts in the field agreed it was just 5 per cent.

Frightening, but it gets worse.

They now all agree it is 1.5 per cent, and it's getting less year on year!

I don't know about you, but I'm going to start using my brain now, before they announce in a few years' time that it's officially proven to be zero.

I will never forget the day I came home and said to my wife, Rosalind, 'I discovered today that I only use 1.5 per cent of my brain.'

She said, 'It doesn't surprise me.'

So what does this mean in real terms that you and I can understand?

It means that we all have the capacity to learn every bible, of every religion, in every language, forwards, backwards and randomly, and still have plenty left for more.

Now, you can use that capacity to improve your memory of: people's faces and names; what you should be doing today and where you should be right now; what happened an hour ago.

Strange, isn't it? We can remember a piece of music we have not heard for ten years and yet we can't remember what we had for breakfast yesterday.

What will seem strange, or at least unusual, is how we can dramatically improve our memories, and how fast we can do it.

Transforming our memories comes down to three things:

1 Our State

You will be able to remember, and recall, far more when you are in a state of relaxation, than when you feel under pressure or stressed. Simply apply some of the techniques in A Deeper Still (page 117) and your memory will improve.

2 Our Belief

Our memories improve the moment we believe they have improved.

It really is as simple as that.

Some people say to themselves (and others), 'I'm hopeless at remembering names.'

And they are.

Most people who want to improve their memories say things like, 'I wish I had a good memory.'

Well, you have. You already have the capacity, the ability and the means. You already have an outstanding memory – right now – and to prove this, decide to remember something.

Don't 'try' or 'attempt' – actually DO it.

Here're some ways:

- **Decide that next time you meet someone new, you will remember their face, their name and one other important fact about them.**

- **Decide that next time you go shopping; you will remember your shopping list without needing to refer to it. Start with a few items, and within a few weeks you will remember your entire shopping list! (If it is an important shop please have your list in your pocket the first and second times. I would hate to think of your guests sitting there eating baked beans when you promised them salmon!)**

And right now:

- **Decide you have a perfect memory.**

Decide it.
  Believe it.
  Know it.
  Why does this work?

It works because we have a conscious and a subconscious. Other than immediate events, our memories are stored in our subconscious. Our subconscious does not judge whether our conscious thought is 'right' or 'wrong' – it simply serves whatever our conscious mind thinks about. So, if we say to someone, 'I am sorry, I am hopeless with names', our subconscious hears this, and proves us right. Equally if we say to ourselves, 'I always remember people's names' . . .

③ What we see and *listen* to, rather than look at and hear.
How often when we look at something, do we really see it?
How often when we hear something, do we really listen to it?

And, how often do we pay the biggest compliment we can to another human being, by paying them total and absolute attention?

Sadly, not as often as we should.

I hate people who generalize (!), however John Gray does it brilliantly in *Men are from Mars, Women are from Venus*, when he talks about how women simply want to share their feelings, they want to talk, and to be listened to, especially at the end of a hard day.

And we men, we want to fix it.

You know how it goes.

Our partners are talking about someone upsetting them at work and we jump in with, 'Well, what do you expect? He's a complete prat.'

Or they tell us about their conflicting diaries – being a mother and juggling other aspects of their lives. And so we buy them a new diary for their next birthday.

At a recent conference, a male delegate took his life into his own hands when, in front of a mainly female audience, he said: 'I get over that one by always phoning my wife from my car when I am driving home. That way she can download everything she wants to say before I get home, and we can enjoy our evening much more.'

I am not sure he got out of the room alive!

Everyone wants to be listened to, to have their feelings at least acknowledged, ideally respected.

Ultimately, if there is one thing that unites all human beings, it's this – we all need to be valued. And listening does just that.

And when we listen, **really listen**, we remember.

When we see, **really see**, we remember.

And finally . . .

When we combine these two, and pay total and absolute attention, we remember the truly important messages being shared with us.

Do it today.

Next time you are on a familiar train journey, take in the scenery – really see it – it will seem like the first time you have ever travelled that way, and the journey will be over in a flash.

When you meet someone new, look at their face, into their eyes, briefly will do, and when they introduce themselves, repeat their name three times, once out loud, then twice silently to yourself, and you will remember it next time.

And with a loved one, next time they speak, turn off the TV, or leave what you are doing, and really listen to them – and show you are doing so. Look into their eyes, through these windows to their soul. You will connect with them on a very deep level.

Let the silences happen. Silences are fine, they are, as they say, golden.

* * *

We remember what is important to us.

We remember what we want to remember.

We remember what we choose to remember.

And when we do take the time to remember, we build closer relationships with other people, because people like to be listened to, and they love to be remembered!

Your choice

You can decide whether to spend all evening helping your child remember dates and events, laboriously . . . or doing it in a few minutes by turning them into an exciting story – happening inside their bedroom.

You can decide whether to read your next presentation from cards or make it come alive by having the use of both your hands!

And you can decide if you want to improve your memory or not.

Two married couples who regularly played bridge together were playing one weekend when they took a break between hands. The wives went out of the room and the following conversation took place:

George: 'You know, Brian, you're doing much better this week as far as remembering what's trump and who played what, and everything.'

Brian: 'Yeah, George, I took one of them memory courses.'

George: 'Really, which one did you take?'

Brian: 'Erm, now let me think. Erm . . . what's it called . . . a red flower . . . got thorns . . . ?'

George: 'A rose?'

THE NAKED LEADER EXPERIENCE

Brian: 'That's it! Rose,' he shouts out of the room to his wife, 'what was the name of that memory course I took?'

If you wish to follow the chapters in the order they were written, please go to Chapter 36, on page 307.

skill teams

Competency frameworks will be the downfall of organizations.

Competency-based training and assessment are finished.

Why?

Firstly, the Boredom Factor – when you hear the word competency, does the blood rush to your head? Does your heart dance with passion and excitement? No, I thought not!

Secondly, because competencies are based on three fundamental and inter-related flaws:

1 **If we work on our 'weaknesses' our strengths will look after themselves.**

2 Everyone must be trained in all of the competencies our organization needs, for us to perform well.

3 People are motivated by all of this stuff.

Wrong!

Sorry, that is unfair.

There is no 'right' or 'wrong' – there is only what takes you closer to what you want to achieve, and what takes you further away.

So, when I say 'wrong' I mean that competencies take you further away from what you want to achieve, because:

1 If we work on our 'weaknesses' our strengths will not look after themselves.

All the evidence now tells us that for our strengths to flourish, and develop further, we have to use and apply them on a regular basis. If we do not, they stagnate. Isn't it strange? We know this of our golf, when we learn a new language, of our hobbies, however we seem to think there are different 'rules' in the world of work. There aren't!

2 Everyone must be trained in all of the competencies our organization needs for us to be a mediocre organization.

So we draw up a list of the competencies we need in an organization:

Here are some examples of current competency lists from two direct competitors – same business, same market, same customer targets:

Organization One	Organization Two
Speed of decision-making	Ability to analyse and interpret information
Ability to think strategically	Agile – able to act in the now
Innovation and out-of-the-box thinking	Understanding of processes
Project management	Programme leadership
Knowledge acquisition	Sharing of knowledge
Planning abilities	Ability to act on instinct
Communication skills	Listening

All very clear then! No possible conflicts, least of all within each organization itself, and everything easy to understand and put into action.

So, to make it slightly more complex, many organizations have different levels of competency requirements for different 'levels' of jobs within the organization (grade/hierarchy). And then within each of these levels, there are several degrees of competency. Again, taking actual words from an actual company:

Aware
Knowledgeable
Proficient

And to take it one final step into the bizarre, the requirement for each of these is not assessed for each person; they are assessed against each **job**!

And the competency-based argument grandly concludes that this system delivers a motivated workforce trained in the total needs of an organization.

Sorry, what it really delivers is a group of general all-rounders, and little more.

It is time to put aside competencies for ever, and focus on the passion, energy and commitment of people.

And to do this, we must focus on their:

- **Wants – Dreams and desires.**

- **Strengths – Gifts and talents.**

- **Value – Their number-one need, to be valued.**

And before you shout, 'But what about the needs of our organization?' remember your people ARE your organization, and if you do not have the right strengths in these people, then either you are in the wrong business or you have the wrong people. Either way, you are doomed, and no competency-based framework will save you.

Empowerment – Permission

Closely linked to competencies is the concept of empowerment.

It is simply not possible to 'empower' another human being, because they are already empowered, and were the very day they were born.

Does your new-born baby need to be empowered to wake up on the hour, every hour? Or to throw up all over your best friend's new dress?

No, of course not.

THE NAKED LEADER EXPERIENCE

Empowerment is one of the saddest jokes we have ever introduced into organizations, because we have used it to mean 'permission'.

And when people, teams and projects await permission, their potential is not being released, nor their talents awakened and used.

And we can do this, by putting together our teams on the basis of their skills.

Skill Teams

What is a Skill Team?

It is a team put together on the basis of the project or task needed, and the skills needed to achieve a successful outcome.

Sounds like any team, what's different here?

Each person is in the team (they are invited to join, or they can apply) on the basis of their number-one skill and strength, provided they enjoy developing and using that skill.

So, for example, you might require a project team that has six defined skill needs:

Outstanding communicator and persuader

Strategy – the big vision

Planning and analysis

Negotiation and influence

Deliverer – someone who always completes and finishes a project

Innovation – someone who can inject fresh and original ideas

So you have six people, who work as a team on all areas, each having one area of expertise on which they will take the lead.

Hang on, that is a recipe for disputes and disagreements.

Putting more than one human being in any team is a recipe for disputes and disagreements. But there is also the possibility of synergy and success. You have to make decisions that will maximize the chance of the latter.

While every skill team has an 'expert', everyone's opinions are to be listened to and valued, and if someone has to force their opinion down others' throats the entire process will fail.

However, when members of the team appreciate the aims of the team and the part they can play, the mutual respect shown between different team members is massive.

After all, you have the person who will be the voice of the team to outside 'stakeholders', as well as someone who will achieve the best possible win-win deals with suppliers, internal and external.

You have the big-picture person – the kind of guy who can share a dream and inspire others to see it and go for it, but who so often then does not know how to implement it . . . well. You have such an implementer in the team too.

Finally, and just as critically, you have the balance between the person who can think of 300 different uses for a paperclip, and who has new ideas when everyone else only sees a brick wall, working alongside the planner – the meticulous, detail-driven, project-spreadsheet-obsessed godsend that every project needs.

Skill teams are so powerful. They allocate people from every talent base needed, to ensure a balance of the right abilities, experience and knowledge. This produces a team that combines 'hard' and 'soft' skills.

Skill teams can be extended to include contractors and

third-party suppliers, and when they have delivered, they disperse.

What's more, many skill teams can operate at the same time, across different projects, departments and traditional hierarchies. It is not a fixed team, in a fixed location.

It is time.

Time to realize that people will do what they want anyway, so we may as well encourage that, and time to unleash the talent, passions and awesome potential of our only asset – our people.

When we do that, we move beyond strategy, and beyond day-to-day work, and we start on what our working lives and organizations must be in the twenty-first century: an exciting adventure.

I invite you to start right away – ask each person in your team to share with each other what they believe their top three skills are, and how these can be best applied for the team or project.

As you discuss this, sit in a circle, in a private room. Respect each other's thoughts and opinions. Feel the positive, constructive and open energy, and enjoy.

With thanks to Malcolm Rose.

If you wish to follow the chapters in the order they were written, please go to Chapter 18, on page 143.

keep your friends close . . .

. . . and your enemies closer.

Are politics and hidden agendas alive and well in your organization?

Yes?

Do you play politics, and have a hidden agenda?

No?

Of course not?

Of course you do!

Please, stay with this – it will transform your career.

Politics

To me, 'politics' in the company sense is simply another word for 'communication'.

So of course you play politics, because you communicate.

And when you communicate, you speak, write and present everything, and that is *everything*, from your own point of you.

How selfish is that?

Totally.

And this is not because you want to stab others in the back, or because you have any ulterior motives, it is because you can do no other.

We can do no other.

We can only ever put forward our own point of view.

We can only ever see the world through our own eyes.

We can only ever know what it is like to be ourselves.

How selfless is that?

Totally.

When we realize this, we put aside the negative meanings of communication, we begin to understand why other people do what they do and most of all, we seek out ways to awaken the leaders inside our people.

Hidden Agendas

Do you ever feel that people are keeping things to themselves?

Do you look at someone and think they have something they are not sharing?

Is your company full of hidden agendas?

Yes, yes and yes again.

And guess what, one of those agendas is yours.

You have a hidden agenda.

Every dream, every action, every fear, every thought, every skill, everything you have about this company, its teams and people that you have – that is your total agenda.

And most of it stays hidden.

Imagine how much information that is, to share with another person – it would be completely impossible, and you wouldn't have the time – and, with respect (which means I am about to show you no respect whatsoever), they would fall asleep after a few hours.

Even if you love someone very deeply, and you spend most of your life with that person, and you speak and connect each and every day and you get to know that person deeper than anyone else, and they know and are as one with you in the same way, you will both share only a fraction of your thoughts, dreams, feelings, fears and lives.

Because only you know what it is like to be you.

And only they know what it is like to be them.

Now, back to your workplace. Imagine a workforce of two, both with hidden agendas.

Now, add a third, then a fourth – the multiple connections of communications that would be needed to open up just a small part of all of these agendas is frightening to even think about.

I tried it once.

I made a huge mistake.

People in one of my teams had been complaining that they had been treated like mushrooms for many years, and I wanted it to be different.

So, I asked my leadership team, including myself, to copy the entire team (sixty-two people) with any and every email and meeting action that were not confidential.

Chaos.

Aside from running out of computer capacity, there was total confusion.

After three days, a woman came up to me and begged, 'Please, treat us like mushrooms again.'

And so I changed things – I said that outstanding

communication comes down to people being able to know where and who to go to, to find something out, and they know they can do this without any fear or favour.

And so, be careful when you think of politics and hidden agendas, everyone has them.

While you know you have a hidden agenda, one of your top priorities is to listen to, share with and inspire from others – their agendas, their hopes, talents, attitudes and dreams.

There will be some people who give politics and hidden agendas a bad name. These people are hell-bent on your destruction in the pursuit of their aims.

They may be bullies – in which case you will know, or soon know, what to do.

They may be 'negs' – people who disagree with any-thing and everything you say, behind your back. Speak with them in public, asking their opinion in front of others (witnesses). Negs thrive when they are ignored, so don't.

And what about the others in your organization and in your life who are only in it for themselves?

The ego-warriors.

How can you, an enlightened warrior, overcome them?

1 Win and retain the loyalty of your people.
   Absolutely essential – do this and you will sleep soundly in bed and enjoy your holidays. This is critical and this book is full of how to do it. So, no excuses.

2 Get a friend in high place.
   Ask your Chief Executive to be your personal mentor. Powerful friends are like gold dust, in particular if you

are looking to release the potential of your people. Ego-warriors don't understand that and will not see any connection between people and profit.

3 **Keep well in with the top influences in your organisation.**
These will include your Chief Executive's Personal Assistant (possibly the most important person in the company), and other PAs. Also, that chap in Underwriting who has been in the same job for over fifteen years – he knows a lot and possibly holds far, far more power than the organization chart may suggest.

4 **Use one of these two tactics for peers:**

•   **Respect them, and give them a standard to live up to.**
Every time you are with them, treat them as your equal in everything you say and do. They will take their guard down and reveal the real them. When they do this, and treat you as their new best friend, hold the relationship there. Do not get any closer, do not drift any further. And while doing this, suggest standards for them to live up to, such as saying, 'What I like about you is you always give other people praise when they deserve it.' Of course, they don't but they should, and they will do!

•   **Confront them.**
Face-to-face, personally and professionally. In private, simply tell them what you have heard that they have said, and ask them if that is true.

They will accept what they said, or deny it.

If they accept it, have a discussion about the issue, not about your relationship with them.

If they deny it, then apologize, saying that you always valued your relationship, and next time your grapevine tells you that this person says something, you will know not to believe it.

Overall, be professional and direct – people will respect you, and your peers will think ten times before taking you out.

Self-esteem

In many ways everything in the Naked Leader books comes down to our self-esteem, our sense of self-value and worth.

People who 'play' politics deliberately for their own agendas at the expense of other people's usually lack self-esteem. However, it is not just them – many leaders I have worked with admit to having low self-esteem.

Too many organizations unwittingly promote low self-esteem by focusing on what is 'wrong' with people or projects. Think about it. Reviews, appraisals, 'risk' meetings. There's always an opportunity to be reminded of what is 'wrong' with us.

High self-esteem is awakened when we remember how amazing we are. And this awakening can happen quietly, privately in a contemplative way. Yes, of course we all have evidence of things we do not do well – things that we struggle to cope with or master. But if we accept these as part of our unique self, we can also accept our many strengths. So please always remember to be your 'self'. Each and every day, be the wonderful, amazing person that you already are. Know this deep inside – know that you are not your low thoughts, you are the highest thoughts you can have. That behaviour you labelled 'bad' in the past was not the true you, and above all, everyone's

opinion of you up to this very moment is based on their
expectations and standards for you, now it is time to set
your own.

If you wish to follow the chapters in the order they were written, please go to Chapter 12, on page 99.

one team – one vision

All teams go through three stages before they can be truly unstoppable. These are:

- **Build Trust.**

- **Reach the Truth.**

- **Be a Team.**

Stage One – Create Total Trust

1.1 The 'givens'

You all WANT to be in this team and to give your best to ensure its success.

As a team you are the people who can make this a success – you need rely on no-one outside the team to achieve your outcome/dream.

1.2   Emphasize that you do not have to 'like each other'

However, you do have to respect each other, and each other's opinions, *especially* when they are different, and sometimes opposing, to yours.

Because if everyone had the same opinion being part of the team would be one of the most boring experiences in life.

1.3   Ask the ultimate question

As a team:

Imagine if we simply could not fail . . .

What would we do?

Where would we go?

Who would we be?

NB: For those who are concerned that this is not 'possible', or engage in a debate on the semantics of the process, ask them just to play along, as if you could not fail.

1.4   Enjoy sharing the responses

And do so in front of each other – if you are a team of under twelve, sit in a circle, with each person sharing their dreams for the team. If it is over twelve, no matter how big, hold at least one session with everyone present, so that everyone's ideas are shared with the group.

And watch the trust, the excitement and unity happen.

Because so often we as teams focus on what could go wrong, what is going wrong, and who is to blame.

Stage Two – Reach the Truth

Openness is mission critical – the more open the debates, the greater your chances of achieving your dream – teams are only really together when they are open.

2.1 Ask each person what is fantastic about working in this team, and for the one thing they would change if they could

This is taking the 'imagine if we simply could not fail' ideas into the day-to-day. Also, many teams and people focus on the second list, and not on what is great about being a part of a team.

Record them on flip-charts, perhaps with the 'fantastic' one with a big smiley face, the other with an unhappy face.

2.2 Identify the priorities – the imperative from the important

You will have two flip-charts, full of the most valuable ideas you need to perform as a team, the key issues, not as dictated by you, but as contributed by the team.

Now, give everyone in the team, including you as leader or facilitator, three votes for each chart (list). Together, as a team (or in separate sessions if you are doing this for more than twelve people), everyone marks three items on each of the charts, that they consider to be the most important and urgent.

After that has been completed, add the scores and identify the most important priorities and actions that are fantastic about being in the team, and that need to be changed. (If there is a tie for votes then include all on the same score, so you may end up with four or five on one or both lists.)

You now have, in one simple exercise:

- Created trust and reached the truth of the issues facing this team.

- Involved the team in identifying these (valued them).

- Identified what can take months to find by other methods.

- The list of things to do more of ('fantastic' list) and those that need action.

Finally, ask for an owner for each of the actions/items – to ensure you as a team do more of the first list and do something different on the second.

And, critically, that 'owner' is accountable to the rest of the team, not to the 'leader', and will update the rest of the team at meetings.

Repeat the same session three months later.

Lessons from Geese

As each goose flaps its wings, it creates an uplift for the others behind it. By flying in a 'V' formation, the whole flock adds 71 per cent greater flying range than if each bird flew alone.

When a goose falls out of formation, it suddenly feels the drag and resistance of trying to fly alone, and quickly gets back into formation to take advantage of the 'lifting power' of the bird immediately in front.

When the lead goose gets tired, it rotates back into the formation and another goose flies at the point position.

The geese in formation honk from behind to encourage those up front to keep up their speed.

When a goose gets sick or wounded or shot down, two geese drop out of formation and follow it down to help and protect it. They stay with it until it is able to fly again or dies. Then they launch out on their own, with another formation, or catch up with the flock.

Lessons from Geese – Team Analysis!

1 **As each goose flaps its wings, it creates an uplift for the others behind it. By flying in a 'V' formation, the whole flock adds 71 per cent greater flying range than if each bird flew alone.**
Lesson: People who share a common direction and sense of community can get where they are going quicker and easier because they are travelling on the thrust of another.

2 **When a goose falls out of formation, it suddenly feels the drag and resistance of trying to fly alone, and quickly gets back into formation to take advantage of the 'lifting power' of the bird immediately in front.**
Lesson: If we have as much sense as the goose, we will stay in formation with those who are headed where we want to go (and be willing to accept their help as well as give ours to others).

3 **When the lead goose gets tired, it rotates back into the formation and another goose flies at the point position.**
Lesson: It pays to take turns doing the hard tasks and sharing leadership – with people, as with geese, we are interdependent on each other.

4 **The geese in formation honk from behind to encourage those up front to keep up their speed.**
Lesson: We need to make sure our honking from behind is encouraging, and not something else.

5 **When a goose gets sick or wounded or shot down, two geese drop out of formation and follow it down to help and protect it. They stay with it until it is able to fly again or dies. Then they launch out on their own, with another formation, or catch up with the flock.**

Lesson: If we have as much sense as geese, we too will stand by each other in difficult times as well as when we are strong.

I wanted to include a completely new and novel approach to team building, I found one . . . and the fact I have included it shows I believe it has merit . . .

Building Teams Using Astrology

Astrology offers methods to describe and explain the specific talents, predispositions, strengths and weaknesses each person brings to the group with whom they work. Equipped with each person's time, date and place of birth, and the open-minded support of those involved, a skilful astrologer can describe the team's dynamics, then say how each individual will contribute to its successes and failures.

After discussing the nature of the project and the technical and personal skills it requires, the astrologer would cast each individual's exact birth map and then discuss it with them. Whether the person has the basic talent, interest and readiness for the project in hand will emerge. Maturely applied, this process leads to teams selecting themselves. Unsuited people find a much better outlet for their talent elsewhere, without counter-productive bad feeling and power struggles. Finally, the whole group meet with the astrologer again to discuss and decide the most effective approach and timing to the work . . .

Such astrological team building can make the best of each person's ability and eradicate many problems that undermine success. It can cut through false expectations and irrelevant goals, allow people to do what makes them happiest. So everyone wins. The project and every team member achieve what they really want.

Roy Gillett, President, Astrological Association of Great Britain.

If you wish to follow the chapters in the order they were written, please go to Chapter 29, on page 245.

the naked truth

Our belief systems are very, very important to us.

Our belief systems determine our reality, our lives and to a very large extent, our very selves.

So, we must choose our beliefs with care.

How does a belief happen?

We may have an idea, an insight, and a fleeting notion. It is not that important to us, it may come and go, however it may develop into an Opinion – which we do not feel too strongly about, until we find evidence to support it, and it becomes a . . .

Belief.

And this is the critical moment – when something becomes a belief.

It can happen at any time.

As Adrian Gilpin of the Institute of Human

Development says, an idea is a table-top, a belief gives it legs.

Do a quick test on your beliefs – complete the following:

People are . . .
Success means . . .
Life is . . .
Money is . .
Love means . . .

For everything we care about, we have a belief, for those things in life that are really important to us, we have deeply held beliefs, or **Convictions**, and once we have such a deeply held belief, it is very, very difficult to shift.

Because we don't want to, and because we don't need to – after all, all of the evidence supports our belief, and conviction.

Every single day, we notice new and ever-more supportive evidence to deepen our belief, and strengthen our conviction.

And from then on, it's self-fulfilling.

Because we are now looking for evidence in all that we do.

Evidence to support what we now know, that we are right. We know we are right, and to prove it . . .

Newspapers know this too well, they know the core beliefs of their readers, and they feed them the same stuff, every day.

Television programmes do this as well.

And so do we, as human beings.

We notice what we choose to notice.

Try this: look around the room, the train carriage or

wherever you are reading this, and take in everything you can see that is red – clothes, wallpaper and cars, whatever.

Now close your eyes for a few seconds – and without opening them, make a mental list of everything you have seen that is blue. How many did you manage?

None? One?

We believe what we see, we see what we believe.

We are like bloodhounds – gathering evidence that supports our view.

Now, of course this does not mean that people never change their views; it simply implies that the more entrenched our beliefs, the more imprinted our views, the harder they are to alter.

Take reading this book.

There will be some things you have read you agree with, other stuff that you don't agree with and some things that you don't feel too strongly about, one way or another.

It's your choice – a choice that is almost totally determined by your conviction because once all this self-fulfilling evidence adds up, the conviction becomes our **Truth**.

It becomes our everyday truth – the way things are, the way things should be, what things mean.

And we start to express our truth, to anyone and everyone who will listen, especially those who agree with us. We love to hear back what we already believe, because it reinforces our being 'right'. (Incidentally, this is the main reason people tend to recruit people they 'like'.)

Listen around you, and most powerfully, listen to yourself, every time you make a statement. Is it an opinion, or a fact?

- **He is a genius.**

- **This is the quickest way.**

- **We are the best football team.**

- ***The Shawshank Redemption* was the best film ever made.**

- **'Cool' is SO yesterday.**

- **All men are hopeless.**

- **This game is the best.**

And we can extend that to many things we think of as real truth, rather than opinion, such as: 'This chair is green.'

Is that a fact or an opinion?

It's an opinion, of course – it's your truth.

If a child was born in a room, and never left that room until it was three, and inside that room there was a chair coloured what you and I would call 'green', and we taught that child that the chair was coloured 'yellow', when the child leaves the room and is shown anything the same colour as that chair, what will they say?

They will say it is 'yellow'.

Are they telling the truth?

Yes, of course they are.

Because they **believe** it to be 'yellow'.

And that is what truth is – what we believe to be the case.

And lying is saying what we **believe** or **know to be** not the case.

We know what we know.

In *Eastenders*, Vicki *lied* to her sister Sharon, telling her that she (Vicki) was pregnant, believing that she was not.

It turned out that she was pregnant.

So, telling Sharon that she was pregnant was a lie, even though she was, just as if she had told Sharon she was not pregnant would have been the truth.

Because it was what she believed, given everything she knew at that moment.

Our beliefs and our truths are very important for many reasons:

- **For ourselves – our belief systems determine so much about our lives, how we feel, and our happiness and inner peace.**

- **For each other – how we react to, and respect others' beliefs is a massive decider in how well we get on with other people.**

- **For our world – for a single reason we will come to very soon.**

Truth and Facts

But what is the difference between a fact and the truth?

I simply don't know.

So I asked some scientists, academics and 'gurus'.

Some said a fact is something on which everyone agrees.

Like, just a few hundred years ago, everyone agreed the world was flat – and if you said otherwise you risked being killed.

Some said a fact is something that can be scientifically proven.

For example, it is scientifically and medically proven that a surgeon washing his or her hands before surgery will reduce the risk of spreading disease.

Everyone knows that.

So why did Hermann Kumell, a medical doctor in Hamburg in the late 1800s, become a laughing stock and practically driven out of his profession, for suggesting that such a practice could save lives?

And the third group said it comes down to the way things actually are, not what we believe about them.

Question: what was the largest island before Australia was discovered?

Answer from these people: Australia.

Isn't hindsight great?

The way things actually are.

Not that simple – because it is we who label things, who give things meaning, and who then say that's the way things actually are.

And so the truth is within us, and all around us, each and every day – it's what we call 'reality'.

At a school where I was speaking, a girl offered me a jelly baby. I took a red one. She looked upset and said: 'You had to take red, didn't you? Reds are the best jelly babies.'

I asked, 'Is that a fact or your opinion?'

'A fact, of course. Everyone knows that, duuuh. Apart from you, but even you know now.'

Indeed, I am now enlightened, I am now a part of a mass of opinion surrounding the world of jelly babies.

And now, back to the biggest question: why is this so important to the future of our world?

Because there is one thing, above all else, that we as human beings must be.

It takes over in discussions; it is the root cause of all arguments, and every war.

It runs across and through every religion, every belief and every cause.

It is one thing that is so important to some people, they willingly risk everything to prove – to be right.

For this:

> [Human beings] will give up love, they will give up peace, they will give up health, harmony and happiness, and they will give up safety, security and even their sanity.

> *The New Revelations – a Conversation with God*
> *Neale Donald Walsch*

To be right.

And, of course, for others to be wrong.

This happens to us every day – people fall out with each other.

In 2003 we had the embarrassing and somewhat ridiculous situation where the British Government disagreed with the British Broadcasting Corporation. As an independent news station reported it: 'Both sides are determined to prove that they are right and the others to be wrong.'

This very public disagreement resulted in the sad death of Dr David Kelly, who many believed was made a scapegoat by the Government.

The usual words that you associate more with a family argument than with governments and respected broadcasters were flying around – you know the ones, the usual, constructive ones:

'Liar'

'You are wrong'

'We demand an apology'

'We'll sue you'

And so it is with people, with different departments and, most powerfully, with nations.

We are right and you are wrong.

And so often, we become like children arguing:

I'm big and you're small,
I'm right and you're wrong
And there's nothing you can do about it.

Matilda
Roald Dahl

And we'll convince you.

And if we can't convince you, we'll prove it.

And if we can't prove it, we'll show you.

And so, we must choose our beliefs with care, whether they serve us, others and the world, well, is up to us.

And we must respect others if they have different beliefs.

How do we do this?

We start by respecting the opinions, beliefs and lives of others. We continue by celebrating the differences we have as human beings, realizing what a boring world it would be if we were all the same, and then, when an event happens, we look at that event from many different angles, from many different perspectives, and ask ourselves the questions:

Which one of these many realities serves me best?
And which serves our team best?
And which serves our world best?

When we do this, we take absolute and total control over our beliefs.

Imagine what the world would look like, then. If we respected the right of others to have different ideas, beliefs, religions, convictions, truths and lives to our own.

It can be this way.

It is in our hands.

It is up to all of us to make it happen.

And when we do, what a different and wonderful world we will live in.

It will be like heaven on earth.

Faith

A chap is walking along a cliff top when he suddenly slips and falls. He frantically reaches out for anything to stop his fall, and he catches a branch that is growing out from the cliff face. He hangs there, and shouts: 'HELP – HELP ME – IS THERE ANYONE OUT THERE?'

No reply.

He shouts again, louder: 'HELP, IS THERE ANYONE OUT THERE?'

Again, no reply.

Just as he is giving up all hope, he says a prayer: 'Oh God, if you are out there, I sure need your help right now.'

To which he hears a very quiet reply, a whisper: 'I am here with you – now, all you have to do is let go of that branch, and I will make sure you do not fall, but are carried gently to your safety on the ground.'

After a pause the man shouts: 'IS THERE ANYONE ELSE OUT THERE?'

With thanks to Steve Noble

If you wish to follow the chapters in the order they were written, please go to Chapter 40, on page 339.

Book Three

Reinvent Your Organization

the business of passion

I often ask at seminars what percentage of our decisions we make on the basis of emotions, and what percentage on logic.

In all areas of our lives.

Over three years, the lowest figure I had for decisions based more on emotion was 60 per cent, with most people going for 80 per cent and higher.

When I think about the world of information technology, I am naturally drawn to the more logical side of thinking and decision-making.

And then I think again.

Most decisions I made as an IT director were made more on emotion – I can never remember selecting a supplier based on logic, certainly not on the basis of their very large replies to our invitations to tender – no-one ever read those.

What I remember is making decisions based on emotions, and then rushing in the logic behind the decision, to justify it after the event.

And that seems to be how we run our lives.

And if it's true for us, it's most definitely true for our people.

And then it happened again, a few weeks later. I once again asked the question:

My reason for raising this is to emphasize the role of emotion in our organizations, and that:

- **People will only ever do something to the best of their ability for one reason, and one reason alone, and that is because they want to.**

- **The process-driven initiatives of the last twenty years seem to have bypassed the fact that people have any emotion completely – resulting in a huge negative backlash.**

- **Many people say they are emotional at home and logical at work.**

So-called logical people will tell us that we only make emotional decisions outside of work, and that while inside a company people revert to making decisions based on the right thing to do, on logical conclusions. Presumably we all leave home in the morning, and as we say goodbye to our partners, children and cats, we hang up our personalities and feelings on the coat-rack, never to wear them again until we return!

Take a look around you as you are reading this – you are unlikely to see much emotion, I grant you, however it is entirely because people are suppressing their true and inner feelings. Isn't that sad? Inside each and every one of us lies an awesome potential, a huge personality and a real person, just waiting to be released. It is our inner feelings, our hearts, our very selves, that companies must engage on-side, if they are to thrive.

Hearts, minds and spirits are the key. When will business leaders realize that the secret of success is simple: harness, ignite and release the power of people?

A Human Resources director told me recently that when people join a company, they are recuited on their apparent logical skills and abilities. When they leave, it is for emotional reasons, to do with who they are. If they are made redundant it is sometimes because of their personalities and inability to get along with others; if they resign it is because of an inner ambition unfulfilled.

We are all living, breathing hotbeds of energy with unique and sometimes extreme ideas and attitudes. That is either a curse or a blessing to your company – it is your choice.

Treat it as an unfortunate trait of your people, and those ideas, feelings and the excitement of being human will remain forever hidden.

Accept it and thrive on it, and you will awaken an energy, a force of giants that has been asleep for perhaps too long.

Emotional Intelligence

Much is written about Emotional Intelligence, it even has its own acronym – EQ, for Emotional Intelligence Quotient.

Considering that so much has been written on the subject, by so many people, few can agree what Emotional

Intelligence actually means, both in terms of definition and importance.

For our purposes, it is defined as this: your degree of awareness of the role of emotions in business.

Most of the tomes on EQ include massive, degree-length papers to measure EQ. Having read many of these, I have drawn out the major areas, but not as a 'test' or any kind of measurement, rather as a tool to consider the key issues for you, your people and your organization.

There follows twenty-one questions, seven each about your own emotional awareness, seven about other people and finally seven on your organization. These are intended for private consideration, and debate with peers, if you so wish.

There are no 'right' or 'wrong' answers, only different choices. These choices reflect your background, your beliefs and your emotional leadership style.

Your Emotional Awareness

One – Emotional Confidence (Self)

1 How visible are you to the people in your organization?
2 What was your most recent, big mistake?
3 What percentage of decisions do you base more on logic than emotion?
4 When you are away from your office, do you ever worry what is happening in your absence?
5 What are your top three strengths?
6 Do you take personal responsibility for anything and everything that happens to you?
7 If you were stripped of your job title and traits of office, would you still be able to get the best from your people?

Two – Emotional Connection (Others)

1   Can you influence people without controlling them?
2   What two top leadership qualities does your next in line have?
3   Can people communicate openly with you, without fear or favour?
4   Can you name fifty people in your company, or customers of your company?
5   Can everyone in your team relate what they do to the dreams of the company?
6   How often does your boss catch you doing something right?
7   When was the last time you had major disagreement, and how was it resolved?

Three – Emotional Company (Organization)

1   What are the three main values in your organization, stated or implied by behaviour?
2   Do your customers love you?
3   Do your meetings buzz with passion?
4   Do you have a mission statement?
5   How many new ideas have your company/team generated in the last twenty-four hours?
6   Do politics and hidden agendas play a big part in your organization?
7   How dependent are you on external suppliers?

Your Emotional Awareness – To think about after you have 'answered' the previous questions

One – Emotional Confidence (Self)

1. *How visible are you to the people in your organization?*
   (Visibility = Charisma. In these times of email, those who communicate in person can communicate with greater impact.)

2. *What was your most recent, big mistake?*
   (Do we admit to making them? Are we honest and open? Whose fault was it?)

3. *What percentage of decisions do you base more on logic than emotion?*
   (Does it matter what labels we give decisions as long as they are true ones?)

4. *When you are away from your office, do you ever worry what is happening in your absence?*
   (An indication of your stress, trust in others to do the job, and belief in your own importance.)

5. *What are your top three strengths?*
   (Some people are very humble! Go on – name them and be proud of them!)

6. *Do you take personal responsibility for anything and everything that happens to you?*
   (Ownership – one of the most powerful and uncomfortable things we can ever do as human beings!)

7. *If you were stripped of your job title and traits of office, would you still be able to get the best from your people?*
   (The acid test of leadership – prove it!)

Two – Emotional Connection (Others)

1   *Can you influence people without controlling them?*
    (Or do people follow you because they have to because of your power and position?)

2   *What two top leadership qualities does your next in line have?*
    (Awareness of a next in line ready to take over with two outstanding qualities – recognition that all the security you need is within you.)

3   *Can people communicate openly with you, without fear or favour?*
    (They will answer yes, so when was the last time someone told you they disagreed – in front of others? We like people who are like us – people who agree with us.)

4   *Can you name fifty people in your company, or customers of your company?*
    (You have the capacity to do this, and your people's names are their favourite sound.)

5   *Can everyone in your team relate what they do to the dreams of the company?*
    (The key motivator for people is to be valued and this is one of the biggest tests of whether they are, or are not – in particular front-line people – e.g. those in call centres or retail stores.)

6   *How often does your boss catch you doing something right?*
    (Are you motivated by pain or pleasure?)

7   *When was the last time you had a major disagreement, and how was it resolved?*
    (Honesty time – recognize that disagreements are great and needed for projects, teams and companies to thrive.)

Three – Emotional Company (Organization)

1   What are the three main values in your organization, stated or implied by behaviour?
    (Do they have values and what do these values mean? Also, are they written or acted on each day?)

2   Do your customers love you?
    (Does your brand make a very strong emotional connection with people? If it doesn't, what can you do to ensure it does?)

3   Do your meetings buzz with passion?
    (Are discussions about football or the weekend full of emotion, but discussions on projects full of boredom? Why?)

4   Do you have a mission statement?
    (If so, what is it, what does it mean, and is it worded to excite the heart and awaken the zest inside an organization?)

5   How many new ideas have your company/team generated in the last twenty-four hours?
    (Leaders are everywhere and the next great big stonking idea is within your people – you are your next Big Idea.)

6   Do politics and hidden agendas play a big part in your organization?
    (The answer is yes – for everyone – we all play politics, which is simply another word for communication, and we all have hidden agendas, which is our own agenda.)

7   How dependent are you on external suppliers?
    (People rarely admit it, but they usually are in some area or other – an awareness of setting people, teams and organizations free to fly by their own wings.)

THE NAKED LEADER EXPERIENCE

If you wish to follow the chapters in the order they were written, please go to Chapter 14, on page 117.

communication power

OK, this is a personal and very powerful strategy which you can act on straight away – it's like a Hitchcock film without the build up, we go straight to the climax.

Four quick starters for ten before we go for it, the cornerstones of Communication Power.

①   Everyone likes to be liked – it is one of our primary desires as human beings. In that respect, we are all the same. In other respects, we may differ wildly in many ways.

Communication Power is all about identifying common bonds and, therefore, what works with everyone. It's also about identifying differences between people to avoid upsetting or disrespecting those we are aiming to communicate with.

2 So, enough about me; tell me about you. What do you think about me? Everyone's favourite subject is themselves. This is not being self-centred, people have no choice. They only know what it is like being themselves, and can therefore only ever speak as themselves.

So, their favourite word in any language in the world is the sound of their own name – learn it and use it (but don't overuse it).

3 When we communicate we do so with our appearance, with touch, movements, and of course with our voice and what we say. Our most dominant expression is our appearance and body language. We often say things without actually saying anything – for example with a certain look.

4 Every time we speak, every time we think, every time we communicate, we do one of three things:
We make a statement
We ask a question
We issue a command

We can combine or confuse all three, or two of the three, and we do this most frequently by making statements and issuing commands, when asking a question, for example:
Are you not in bed yet? (A command posing as a question).
Are you being deliberately stupid? (A statement pretending to be a question).

Conversation Power – Fifteen Powerful Examples

1   Lying
How to spot a liar

1   No eye contact. His eyes will look away. If the room has a door – that's where they'll look.
2   Crossing of arms and/or legs (defensive).
3   Their eyes will narrow.
4   Hands on the face, especially the mouth. This is an attempt to conceal or cover.
5   Sometimes the head will nod a 'no' when answering a 'yes' question, or vice versa. This is a subconscious movement.
6   Mispronouncing words or mumbling.
7   Overstated friendliness/laughing. He wants you to believe, and he wants you to like him so you will believe him.
8   Too much detail.
9   Filling every silence in the conversation.

How to avoid being lied to

1   Sit in the higher chair to elevate yourself and literally take the higher ground. A subtle tactic.
2   Uncross your legs, and open your arms and lean back. Make yourself 'open' to the truth – but take care not to look too confident or you will give yourself away!
3   Ask for specific details (a direct challenge to the liar).
4   Keep direct eye contact (it invites them to tell you the truth).
5   Invade their personal space. Get close; they'll get uncomfortable.

6 Give them an 'out'. Make it easy for them to tell the truth. [Pretend you didn't hear them correctly or tell them you didn't understand what they said. Always leave a way out so they can change their words and tell the truth without losing face.]

7 Stay calm. Never show surprise or shock. Treat everything they say with the same level of acceptance. If you react negatively you will lose any chance of being told the truth.

2 How to Communicate with a Teenager

- **Listen with your lips shut.**

- **Do not be judgemental when you're listening (it's harder to do this than you might imagine).**

- **Train your mind to respond – NOT to react.**

- **Stop what you are doing. Turn around so that your heart is facing your teenager's heart (it doesn't have to be obvious that you are doing it). Research shows that most mothers and fathers hold their babies close to their heart, in order to connect and to comfort their child.**

- **Listen from *their* point of view; it's about them, not about you. And don't always come up with rescue solutions to their problems. Sometimes they just want to talk.**

The key here is to ask them now and then if they think that you are listening to them. And don't give up on this, you'll get better and better and it's a lifetime exercise.

And with teenagers, always remember these three golden rules:

- **If it's important to them, it's important to you.**

- **Their number-one desire, by far, is approval and respect from their peers.**

- **Just like with adults, they are not always their behaviour.**

Thanks to Cim Bartlet

3 Listen
On Listening
By Ralph Roughton

When I ask you to listen to me and you start by giving me advice, you have not done what I have asked.

When I ask you to listen to me and you begin by telling me why I shouldn't feel that way, you are trampling on my feelings.

When I ask you to listen to me and you feel you have to solve my problems, you have failed me, strange as it may seem.

Listen!

All I ask is that you listen, not talk or do. . . just hear me. When you do something for me that I can do for myself, you contribute to my fear and inadequacy.

And I can do for myself. I'm not helpless.

Maybe discouraged and faltering, but not helpless.

But, when you accept as simple fact that I do feel what I feel, no matter how irrational, then I can quit trying to convince you and get about the business of understanding what's behind this irrational feeling.

And when that's clear, the answers are obvious – and I don't need advice.

Irrational feelings make sense when we understand what is behind them.

Perhaps that's why prayer works, sometimes, for some people . . . because God is mute, and doesn't give advice or try to fix things.

God just listens and lets you work it out for yourself.

So, please listen and just hear me. And if you want to talk wait a minute for your turn and I will gladly listen to you.

Thanks to Judith Underhill – Your Business Matters
www.your-business-matters.com

4   How to Handle a Cynic

Note: sceptics and cynics are very different animals.

A sceptic keeps an open mind; a cynic will disagree with almost everything you say.

About one in ten people fall into the 'cynic' category. You've been there with them, and boy are they drains. Turn them round by agreeing with them!

A real example of using reverse psychology with a cynic:

> Cynic: 'That tennis club is not right for me, it would be a waste of time me joining.'
> Persuader: 'Oh, I think it's great.'
> Cynic: 'NO, it's NOT, it's appalling.'
> Persuaded: 'Oh, well if you feel that strongly, don't join.'
> (Pause)

THE NAKED LEADER EXPERIENCE

Cynic: 'I'm not saying I would never join.'

Persuader: 'No way, it sounds dreadful. If I was you I would not join.'

Cynic: 'It's not that bad, there is a nice pool.'

Persuader: 'No, I'm convinced joining should be the last thing you do.'

Cynic: 'Well, I don't agree, I'm going down there tomorrow.'

5 When Presenting, Speak from the Heart

When we speak from the heart, other hearts listen.

In one week, across three different conferences, I had three experiences that all added up to one thought . . .

1 I saw James DeWatteville at National Grid Transco Information Systems hold the audience in the palm of his hand, with a brilliant personal story at the start of his presentation:

'I was travelling home to Andover from Waterloo. I sat down, and a young chap sat opposite me. We exchanged brief looks as one does, and I noticed he had two cans of Stella, a copy of *FHM* and a novel. Anyway, I sat back and snoozed. I woke suddenly when we arrived in Andover. I rushed to get off, and as I did so this guy opposite me did the same. But in his hurry he left behind all his stuff. So I quickly grabbed his lager, magazine and book and hurried off the train.

When I got on the platform I looked around for him and he wasn't there! It was only when the doors closed behind me that I realized what had happened, he had not been getting off at all, had gone to the loo. And there I was, holding this chap's belongings . . .'

2 Next day, a keynote presentation, company name withheld! Chief Executive standing behind lectern reading from paper and slides. Business Power-Point presentation, very busy slide one, even busier slide two, room nodding off. Suddenly a hand went up, and a question was asked: 'Does the company have any plans to make people redundant this year?'

(Pause.)

CEO comes out from behind lectern and with no notes. He walks to the front of the stage and makes direct eye-contact with the audience. He makes an impassioned speech from his heart, about how things are tough, how-ever if they are to downsize it will be done differently from before. It will not hide behind any process or consultancy initiatives; it will be done very openly from the start. He then said four words that stunned everyone in the room, including me.

'**I am very sorry** for all the heartache, anguish and uncertainty that I have personally caused you in the past – of course, I have to make difficult decisions, and in the future I promise you I will make them in a different way.'

3 End of the week in Cardiff. Looks like an all-day Power-Point again. Chairman of conference (and com-pany) stands up at the beginning, puts his notes to one side, and says (names changes): 'Before we begin, as many of you will know, Martin McCarthy finally lost his battle against cancer on Sunday, and left this world. Our love and best wishes go to his family, Clare, Elizabeth and Lorna. Please join me in a few moments' reflection for Martin and his loved ones.'

Three unconnected, unprompted and unexpected events, that all add up to one thing:

When we speak with a group of people, be it our team, our company or at a conference, the most powerful way to get any and every message across is to be ourselves, and speak from our hearts. This might be with a personal story or experience, sharing our genuine thoughts, or capturing the feeling in a room.

Whatever it is, when we do it, we put aside preparation, politics and paper, and communicate directly with people's real selves.

And we can do that for everything we want to get across, as much for a business message and team presentation, as for a personal story, a sincere feeling or a sad reflection. Two key reasons:

- When we speak from the heart, other hearts listen.
- Bin the Power-Point.

6   How to Get Someone to *Know* What They Think They Don't

Ask a question. If they reply 'I don't know' ask: 'If you did know, what would you say?'

Here are two real examples.

From a leadership workshop:

A: 'What would you like to achieve in your life?'
B: 'I don't know.'
A: 'But if you did know, what would it be?'
B: 'Oh, if I knew, it would be happiness, total inner peace.'

And, from BBC Radio 4's programme, *The Commission*, discussing food and fat:

Me: 'What one thing, above all others, would you recommend that people do with regard to the food they eat?'

Expert: 'I don't think there is one thing that is more important than anything else.'

Me: 'But if there was one thing, what would it be?'

Expert: 'Oh, if there was one thing, it would be to enjoy your food.'

(This is one of the very few times 'but' is a wonderful word – it interrupts their pattern of thinking.)

7 How to Handle Three Negative Phrases You Will Face

1 'You have to have the lows, to experience the highs.'
It's all relative, if you decide never to have lows – replacing them with lessons – imagine how high those highs will be.

2 'This is all just positive thinking, and positive thinking doesn't work.'
Actually, it's more than positive thinking. But if it was just positive thinking, that gives us a choice – we can be positive or negative each and every day.

If you think living is all about lowering your head, hunching your shoulders and expecting the worst to happen in each and every moment, great. If not, great as well – it's your life.

3 'That's just wishful thinking.'
Absolutely. Ask the person who said this if they had one wish in life, what it would be – they will probably tell you!

8 No-one Can Make You Sad Without Your Consent, But These Phrases Have a Good Go . . .

❶ 'I don't want an argument' or 'I don't want to argue with you,' or similar.
Oh yes you do, and that's exactly what you're going to get.

❷ 'Look what you've made me do' or 'You make me feel really guilty' or similar.
No-one else can make you feel anything, except yourself.

When we discover this, we take ownership, and life will keep encouraging us to discover this over and over again until we finally choose to do so.

❸ 'You're being very defensive' or similar.
Eh – if they are getting defensive, maybe it's because they feel they are being attacked. And if there is a phrase guaranteed *to make someone feel defensive, this is it. And finally, defensive is no bad thing, it's simply a survival mechanism.*

9 Less is More

A gesture, a look, one single action or word, can speak volumes. (Watch *Rain Man* – towards the end where Dustin Hoffman puts his head on the shoulder of Tom Cruise).

10 How to Network a Crowded Room

Walk up to a group of three people talking, and move in between two of them, staying just behind an invisible line that would be drawn between them. They will both move slightly back to invite you into the circle. The speaker may stop – in which case say: 'I am sorry to interrupt you, my name is [your name in full].' Shake hands with all of them, and then say to the person who was speaking, 'Sorry, please carry on.'

Listen and then ask a question when you can.

And to move on to the next group, say, 'It's been great talking with you, thank you,' and walk away.

Or, 'Will you excuse me please?'

Or, 'Do excuse me, please.'

11 Spreading Your Message Like Wildfire

Identify the key influencers in your organization – and ensure they buy into the message. It will save you a lot of time, as they spread the message around. If these people are with you, you have a greater chance of the vast majority being with you.

Communication spreading depends on very few individuals.

Of course, get the message wrong and the grapevine will strangle your message, not help it grow.

The alternative way to spread your message was learnt from personal experience. I was misquoted in a computer magazine once, and what they printed was not very complimentary about the company I was working for! Rather than not mention anything and allow it to blow over, my boss sent an email to the whole department, which basically told them not to read this article, under any circumstances. Needless to say it became the hottest property of the day!

12 How to Say Sorry Without Saying Sorry

Many people do not apologize enough, others do it all the time. When something happens that you are sorry about, but feel it isn't necessarily your place to apologize, try saying:

'I am very sorry that [the event] happened.'

Depersonalize the situation. Apologize for the event, not for you.

13 Petrty SamrL

Accodrnig to rscheearch at an Elingsh uinervtisy, it deosn't mttaer in waht oredr the ltteers in a wrod are, the amy iprmoetnt tiling is taht fist and lsat itteer is at the rghit pclae. The rset can be a toad mses and you can sitil raed **it** wouthit porbeim. Tihs is bcuseae we do not raed ervey iteter by it slef but the wrod is a wiohe.

Seomtihng to thnik abuot . . .

With thanks to Steve Rock

14 Make Sure They Are Ready to Receive

The impact of any communication depends on how ready your receiver is to listen to, take in, acknowledge, understand and act on the message. It is very important to appreciate what 'state' people are in when you send out the message. Let us all learn from David Brent in *The Office* who told his team he had bad news and good news – the bad news was that the office was closing and everyone would either lose their jobs or be relocated. The good news was that he (David) was being promoted!

Ensure your people, or indeed the other person is ready to receive.

With thanks to Martin Humphries

15 Lose Your Reserve

And truly connect with everyone you meet – even if they are a 'stranger'.

Pedro

The crossword face on a man my age,
An anomalous channel from eyes to laughter
Dipping below the skyline where his battered
Hat shadows his face.

Picture the deft hands folding the tobacco leaves,
A string in his mouth, tep-tethering the shank,
Smooth-rolling along the leg of his trousers,
And sitting, sitting in a tobacco-rolling stance,
And the delicate intertwining fingers of a man
Who had ploughed a field with an ox when I first
Came on him, and I helped to clean the blade,
And clean the ox in the stream, and tie her up
With jagged rope to an iron in the ground.

Picture this man who offers fruit juice with rum
To another man who has walked over a hill,
Shows, when asked, how a cigar is folded,
Then breaks it when I ask to smoke it—
'Too young, come'—
And takes out pencil-thin cigars he folded last year,
And we have a smoke.
Few words to caulk the sense of it.

Picture these two men communicating with poor
    Spanish
On one side and no English on the other,
Just talking and pointing and laughing like old mates,

Like young children do with foreign children—
When do we gain reserve? When did I lose it?
I lost it on a hill in Cuba when I came over a rise
And met Pedro, a man of my own age.

By Maurice Spillane, written specially for this book

And, finally, my three favourite miscommunications:

3rd A quote from a newspaper interview:

> *'Using people's first names is very important,' stressed Taylor.*

2nd Letter from a hotel:

> *Here we are at the start of a new millennium with many exciting projects ahead, the most exciting one of which will be our closure at the end of September, for approximately six months.*

And in first place, a household-name company that must think its staff are stupid. And this is a real example!

Extract (name changed!)

> *To All Staff*
> *As you know we have been carrying out an independent review of our Marketing operations. This study has been carried out by Michael Blake, the Operations Director of Michael Blake Marketing.*
> *I am pleased to tell you that study is now completed. Its main recommendation is that we need to strengthen our marketing with the appointment of a new Marketing Director.*

I have decided to accept Michael's recommendation on this, and it is with great pleasure that I announce the formation of a new Marketing Strategy Department, to be headed by the following new appointment as Marketing Director: Michael Blake.

If you wish to follow the chapters in the order they were written, please go to Chapter 11, on page 95.

THE NAKED LEADER EXPERIENCE

those who live by the sword . . .

. . . will be shot by those who don't!

You may have seen the James Cameron film, *Titanic*. You may have seen it more than once. (Why? It sinks every time.)

I discovered recently that the film is based on a true story.

So, why did the real *Titanic* sink?

It did hit an iceberg, and that definitely played a part in its demise.

But why did it hit the iceberg? Because it was not *agile*, not *fast moving* enough to turn in time.

From the moment the crow's-nest phoned down to the bridge and they had that historic exchange:

Bridge: 'What do you see?'
Crow's-nest: 'Iceberg – right ahead.'

The passengers', crew's and vessel's fate were sealed, because the ship was too big and its rudder too small to turn it in time.

Like too many organizations today.

One of the main reasons for this is because there is so much work to be done – we seem to have more stuff to do than ever, with always fewer resources.

Projects	with less	People
Marketing	with less	Clarity
Technology	with less	Application
Complexity	with less	Tolerance for error
Delivery	with less	Time
Methodology	with less	Innovation
Research	with less	Money

So, how can we ensure we are agile enough to thrive and survive in the twenty-first century, and most importantly, ensure our agility is focused on our customers?

Firstly we must understand the context of this new century, of this new business age:

The Next Business Age – When the Customer is King, Queen and all the other members of court as well

1   Matter Matters Less
The new value of a company is to be found in intangibles: people, ideas, information.

2   Space – Distance Just Collapsed
The web just made you global, day one, and right next to each and every customer.

3   Time – Tomorrow Just Arrived
You can now reach anyone, anytime.

4   People – Your Crown Jewels
They are your last, final and most powerful unique selling resource.

5   Growth – Be a Pioneer
The advantages of being first in your market, with a new product or service, are greater than ever.

6   Markets – Buyers Have the Power
Make sure it is easy for your customers to buy from you, twenty-four hours a day.

7   Transactions – With Every Sale, Contract and Contact
You are dealing one-to-one with your customer – make sure you treat them as if they are really special, because they are. They are your livelihood!

The Agile Company

Everyone in business is talking about the Agile Company.

What is it? What does it mean? What does it look like?

In my view, there are ten key features – in order of priority:

① People at the front line must be able to make the decisions they need to, to delight customers.

Warning Sign – somebody in Customer Service on the phone seeking permission to help a customer, with that customer right in front of them, hearing every word!

② Everything in your company is geared towards customer service.

You therefore value people, inspiration and motivation very highly – it will be your people's passion and persona that will determine, in your customers' eyes, if you are a trusted company.

Beware – especially in shops – overheard discussions about how appalling the company is to work for (and don't tell people not to do this or they will do it all the more. Motivate them).

③ Company hierarchies must be accompanied by clear ownership statements – 'The buck stops here.'

Organizational charts are pointless if there is no indication of who does what.

④ You make fast and true decisions.

Put a time limit on the decision, and then take it with the information you have, closing off all other options and possibilities.

5 **Everyone in the company knows the big picture, where they fit in and how they play a part in overall success.**
Know where you are going and what you are about, and share it with everyone, that's everyone. This is the best way to put an end to 'us and them'. And ban terms such as 'back office'. There is no such thing.

6 **Know where the knowledge sits, and moves around.**
It's inside people's heads, and people walk around, and walk away. Do a quick survey of your people; when you want to find something out, who do you go to? You will be amazed by the small number of people who hold all of the knowledge. These people are critical to you and your future.

7 **People from Head Office spend time on the front line.**
Tesco do this regularly, and with outstanding results. A senior manager will be a shelf-stacker for two weeks; the HR director will go on the tills to pack customers' bags, etc. It is a powerful way to understand what your company actually does, and what is going right and wrong.

8 **Use email replies to best advantage.**
Avoid 'reply to all' as much as you can. Set up a central email depositary to copy to, which can be visited by your peers to see all emails that have been sent.

9 **Be as flexible as you can about the needs of your people.**
Show understanding after a bereavement, extend maternity leave, perhaps allowing the new mother to work from home, and be as flexible with working hours as you can. This kind of trust and flexibility will result in people working harder, and you will get a massive return for showing you value your people.

🔟 Understand that you are all totally dispensable.

Oh dear – major decision to be made and he/she is on holiday – don't let it happen. And if you as a manager/supervisor/whatever believe that your true value lies in you being indispensable, consider an alternative. Your true value, your talents and strengths, your success now and in the future, lies within you, not with a job you happen to be doing, right now.

Don't believe me? Fine, make yourself indispensable. These days it's the fastest way to being dispensable, because people who think they are, and tell others they are, usually are not.

A real agile experience under very unexpected and almost unbearable circumstances:

We were on a conference call to New York, when the call was suddenly broken off. A plane had flown into the World Trade Centre. Our company had over 500 people in those two towers.

We watched the full horror unfold on TV, and saw a second plane hit the other tower. Amid all of the care and compassion, we knew we were in the middle of the worst Disaster Recovery case anyone could ever face. It seemed so unreal.

Fighting back the tears, we realized that the immediate back-up system to the North Tower was in the South Tower (it was never conceived possible that both towers would ever be destroyed at once, indeed, only one was insured).

We lost most of our team in New York. Everything else seemed unimportant, however somehow we kept going.

We let everyone in the company in the US know that we were going to hold Disaster Recovery conference call meetings every day at 6.00 p.m. UK time. This was done using word of mouth, mobile phones, faxes, private emails and home numbers, etc.

Everything we did was based on what seemed to be the right thing to do, ranging from priority systems to be recovered, where they would be recovered (both towers had gone), understanding the skills left in the company, ascertaining the fate of colleagues, while liaising with Human Resources as they responded to families and friends of the lost/missing.

It's also at these times one realizes how resilient human beings are, and how everyone pulls together and will do WHATEVER it takes to get the job done . . . which every-one did!

We started every call with everyone on the call intro-ducing themselves . . . as people joined who we had thought were dead, the emotions were beyond description.

The first system recovered was email, and was con-sidered to be the number-one priority. Indeed, it was thanks to the power of email that so much communication and information passed so quickly after the event, for all companies and families involved.

One minute I was talking to my colleagues on the ninety-sixth floor of the North Tower, the next most were dead. Between us, we attended some ninety memorial services for lost colleagues.

David, I share this story not to show how clever we were, or to share what we did, which was whatever we could. I share it in the hope that no-one, not one single human being, has to ever again go through what my friends and colleagues in the United States suffered on that day.

I hope people will understand that I don't share my or

my company's name as they are totally irrelevant. All I will say is we all value each other a lot more now, every single day, as well as knowing that when human beings pull together, they can achieve anything, in any situation, and in any time scale.

If you wish to follow the chapters in the order they were written, please go to Chapter 7, on page 67.

change leadership

'It's time for *Teletubbies*' is one of the most familiar, and wonderful phrases to our children. One of the most successful children's programmes in the world, our little ones have been captivated by Tinky Winky, Laa-laa, Dipsy and Po for many, many hours. Every day their adventures excite millions of young imaginations with their amazing and unusual adventures that have you on the edge of your seat . . . or not.

Yet, with all due respect to everyone involved, in my opinion every *Teletubbies* transmission is totally predictable and formulaic.

And therein lies its success, and the biggest proof that we as human beings like to be comfortable, to know what is happening. And as this programme demonstrates, this characteristic develops in us at a very early age.

Every time we visit this familiar land of rabbits, flowers and very green grass, our experience is virtually the same.

The same start, the same ending, and most crucially the same format in the middle, which the programme shows, twice. That's right – exactly the same sequence, 'again, again, again.'

What a rip-off, I remember thinking, the first time I saw this.

And then I looked at the youngsters watching, and the viewing figures – children everywhere were glued to the screens, feeling very happy, certain and content, especially on the second showing.

Because they had already seen it, the repeated story was familiar to them, and young children love familiarity – it makes them feel comfortable, safe and secure. Children need to feel this way to feel at peace with themselves, with their families and at one with the world. And so do we all.

It is not just children who need these feelings – adults do as well. Our inner selves (the real us) seek out such feelings all of our lives. No matter how much our outer selves (the selves we put on show to other people) pretend otherwise.

There is not some magic age at which our maturity tells us to abandon everything familiar. Of course as teenagers we rebel against things we know, and all our lives we seek out adventure and excitement, but we always need a giant elastic band around us to pull us back to where we feel we 'belong' – deep down everyone craves to feel safe. Yes, we need to take risks, and we will do when we choose to, however we also need to know where we stand, and how we fit in with everything around us.

It is a paradox.

We want freedom, excitement and fun, yet most of us

need to feel in control of our experiences. Even if what we are doing, such as riding a rollercoaster, makes us feel out of control. As long as we have made that choice, and it is not forced on us by another, that is fine.

This applies as much in our working lives as it does in our personal lives. We do not hang up our personalities at the front door as we leave for work – although at times we like to pretend we do.

And so the familiar drifts ever deeper into our companies . . .

Think about the guidance we are given when making presentations:

> 'Tell them what you are going to tell them, then tell them, then tell them what you told them.'

We are simply not comfortable with change. If you do not believe me:

- **Turn someone's desk round to face a different direction when they are on holiday.**

- **Change your newspaper and see how long it takes you to navigate the news format and layout.**

- **Rotate where you sit at the dinner table, as a family.**

Change causes confusion, even chaos, in our minds.

When human beings are faced with such a situation, we automatically look for the fastest and simplest way out.

Inside, we scream for clarity.

For example, if your manager was to tell your manager's manager (their manager) that you are not as good at your job as you once were, what would you expect them to say?

Now – read that sentence again.

Any clearer? No, of course not. It is totally unclear, appalling grammar and full of different meanings. The last 'them' in the sentence could refer to your manager or your manager's manager, or a part of your mind might read 'them' as all the four managers previously mentioned, who were in fact just two people!

And when you finished the sentence, you were seeking that very clarity – and you got it – by being asked very simply to read the sentence again. Which you probably did.

We all understand that, and unless you got yourself in a loop of rereading the same two sentences over and over (in which case you will not have reached this part by now!) you moved on none the wiser . . .

This principle of clarity over confusion is used by police teams when they carry out a raid. Next time you hold an illegal drugs party, watch what happens.

You hear nothing, everything is normal, and then all hell breaks loose. First the smoke comes through the windows (confusion), followed moments later by burly men crashing through doors and windows (chaos). The people in the room are by now desperate for clarity, so when a clear instruction comes:

> 'GET DOWN!'
> 'GET DOWN!'
> 'GET DOWN!'

they obey, automatically.

It would not work if they shouted, amid the smoke, noise and mayhem: 'Good evening, ladies and gentlemen, my name is Sergeant Mike Thomas from the local Special Weapons and Tactical Unit – SWAT for short – and I would like you all to gather next to the back door ready to introduce yourselves, in alphabetical order.'

'What was that? What are we supposed to do?'

We don't like surprises, and once they happen, we look for normality, and we need it fast.

We don't like projects being late – we look for an easy explanation, and the simplest is to blame someone else – it is quick, easy and gets the blame for something we do not understand away from us.

We like to know what is going on – people list being involved in decision-making and being valued as top personal motivators, so when we keep them in the dark, the grapevine takes over. And of course the grapevine proves correct, so very often (because someone somewhere will tell someone else what is happening because we love to prove to other people we know something they don't – it gives us power over them).

And yet all organizations look for faster ways of changing, of keeping pace with the market, proclaiming that 'change is the norm' and 'the only constant is change' and even 'the nature of change is changing'.

Such joy!

There is a dilemma here. Our organizations seek out ever more change, yet we as human beings do not like change – and what is our organization if not us? What is any organization if not its people?

So, what's the answer to this dilemma?

My belief is this. We do not like other people changing us, but we love to change other people.

Think about it.

How often do we hear people say 'X is not good with

change', or 'Y needs to be more comfortable with change' yet how little we hear those people saying 'I don't like change', for fear of appearing weak or staid?

In fact, the only way to overcome resistance to change is to avoid the resistance in the first place, and win the buy-in of our people . . . we do that when we:

> Don't talk about change, we talk about choice.
> Avoid confusion, and always go for clarity.

And above all, give them choice, freedom and authority and they will deliver for you, every time.

They will choose to give and to be their very best, they will be ready for anything, and will make choices accordingly.

The Seven Keys to Overcoming Resistance to Change (and encouraging people to make Choices)

1 True Leadership
Having the courage and the ability to inspire.

2 Vision – the Dream
Be clear, concise and compelling.

3 Ownership
Ensure that everyone feels part ownership of the dream or project.

4 Strengths
Play to people's strengths, gifts and passions.

5 Freedom
People need to feel free to operate within clear guidelines.

6 Communication
Foster informal and open debate – free of blame.

7 Persistence
Keep going when all around have fallen by the wayside.

John Bird is the founder of The Big Issue, *the magazine sold by homeless people to help give them real involvement in the community, pride and self-sufficiency. In his normal direct style, he shared with me how he helped others to take ownership and responsibility:*

Most Leadership Stinks
I am supposed to be a good leader. Really, I'm not. I leave others to take the lead. But they all come back to me for benediction. They need my blessing. Because they need my blessing I realize that I have done something wrong. I'd like to explore what I've got wrong.

I started my leadership life late in life. I was forty-five. Up until then I had never employed anyone other than my mate and his girlfriend. They often didn't turn up.

So you could say that at forty-five I was on a hiding to nothing, having never been an employer. Then The Big Issue.

All my skills were around my own odyssey, of getting through, of overcoming aggression, prison, ignorance. Everything I did, I did around myself. Then I found I was leading a load of people who didn't know what to do next.

So I had this acute sense of survival and achievement that was all to do with me. And suddenly there were all these dependent folk. I loathed them. I despised their supplicancy, their letting me lord it over them. I felt like Wyndham Lewis, the fascist writer and painter, who as an officer in the First World War said his working-class soldiers were like girls because they were so compliant. He loathed their acceptance of everything.

I struggled for a few years with my, at times, bestial outbursts at my staff. I couldn't respect anyone. I was it.

Fortunately I began to become less loathing of others because I began to realize that fear couldn't last for ever. But it was a moderating of my fascist tendencies. I began to listen. I began to become more of a diplomat. I saw the power of saying to people what they wanted to hear.

I got people who were more house-trained than me.

What I have come to understand, coming from such an oppressive concept of leadership, is that you have to get everyone to take the lead. They who turn off the photocopier, they who report the lack of toilet paper in cubicle 3, they who pick up the Coke can on the stairs are all expressing a kind of leadership. A hands-on leadership. A private but public leadership. An 'I'm not waiting for you to take the lead; I'm doing it myself' leadership. It is the best of kinds. It is the deepest of kinds.

The big bitch/bloke at the head is shite. They can certainly bring people together. But unless you get everyone doing the small incremental things in an organization then you have failed.

Our current leaders are no good at building a better world. It will come from the ordinary people taking the lead, not waiting for the nostrums of the mighty.

If you wish to follow the chapters in the order they were written, please go to Chapter 31, on page 271.

THE NAKED LEADER EXPERIENCE

your customers hate . . .

. . . to be sold to, but they LOVE to buy.

Just like you and me.

Yet, when will shops and services understand this? How many more door-to-door calls? How much more spam? Why must we run the gauntlet of the aggressive street charity collectors, the 'do you have a loyalty card?' question every time we make a purchase (when real loyalty comes from shopping there without one!) and the 'extended warranty' sell (on something we have been assured is the best in the market)?

In every area of our personal and business lives, we are being bombarded.

Whole professions have developed their own images around this, deserved or not. What values, styles of selling and experiences come to your mind when you think of:

Estate Agents?
Double-glazing Salesmen?
Car Salesmen?

Do you think 'con-men', or well-informed professionals? It's more likely to be the former.

Why? Perhaps because these groups of people often complicate and confuse what they are selling, and are also very pushy at selling.

I remember a few years ago I wanted to buy a shower. Simple enough. The shower representative came to my house (my big mistake). I had already made up my mind, but he was determined that I should buy a more expensive model and started spouting off about its 'embedded technology' (his big mistake).

Initially I listened politely and then returned to the model I had chosen, but he was undeterred. And so I asked him what all of the technology he had been talking about, and the microchips he seemed to know by name, actually did, in detail.

No, he did not know, but he found them very impressive. Sadly for him, he lost the sale.

Some shops do everything they can to keep us out. Indeed, almost every small shop in London has the following sign in a prominent position:

'No change given for any reasons, unless a purchase is made'.

I saw this sign in a London shop recently, which turned most similar signs on their heads:

THE NAKED LEADER EXPERIENCE

Welcome

We give change for anything and everything
And you do not have to buy anything.

A very clever sign. In the words of the shop owner: 'We used to have a sign that said the opposite – which in effect said, "Go away." Now, we attract over three times more people into our shop, and because we tell them they don't have to buy anything, most of them do.'

As human beings we have this natural, in-built mechanism (there since we were children) called reciprocity, which basically says you do something for me and I'll return the favour.

And there is no difference in our working lives. Remember, we hate to be sold to, we love to buy. And that is true of everything we have to sell – which may be a product, an idea or our 'self'.

So, revisit your service or product. How is it promoted – in words that suit your marketing department or in words that suit your customer?

Successful selling comes down to mastering the art of rapport building, relationships and trust – in other words, creating the right environment for the other person to buy.

Here are the seven 'Be's for business-to-business selling, many of which can be translated into every successful sales situation:

1. **Be Prepared.** Read up about the company you are meeting. Take an hour before each meeting to memorize this. Know your potential customer better than they know themselves. How? Study their website – very few companies know their website very well, even if they have developed it themselves.

2 **Be Emotional.** Translating what you do into real bottom-line value for them, as opposed to the product details, is one thing, now we need to add emotion. Do this by asking yourselves 'so what?' at every stage.

A real example – a shortened version of how Harley Davidson changed their marketing to focus on the experience and not the bike . . .

    'We make motorbikes.'
    'SO WHAT?'
    'They will last for many years, never let you down and they look great.'
    'SO WHAT?'
    'They look great, you look great.'
    'SO WHAT?'
    'Well, you can escape your boring job, dress in black leather, hit the open road of freedom, and have members of the opposite sex stare at you in awe as you drive past.'
    'SOLD!'

Question: Do your customers LOVE you? Do they tattoo the name of your company on their shoulders? Harley Davidson customers do. What strategies can you think of to get your customers to feel this way?

3 **Be Honest.** If you cannot meet any of the needs being discussed, say so, and end the meeting there and then. You will be remembered for ever – and called again when the time is right.

4 **Be Personal.** People buy from people, and the person you are with will decide if they like you within three seconds. Their attention span will be thirty seconds, at most, so impress them early! To buy from you they must trust and respect you, to buy lots from you they must like you, end of story.

5 **Be Quiet.** Listen and ask questions. Let the other person talk about their favourite subject, themselves. Answer their main question – 'What's in it for me?' Read their body language like a book, this way you will identify their top personal buy-buttons, which will always be emotional and will be linked to one of four:

  - **Influence – will it give the buyer great personal influence in their team or organization?**

  - **Answers – does it answer a specific, real and painful problem being faced by the buyer – and in solving the challenge, will it make the buyer look a hero?**

  - **Time – will it save the buyer time – their most precious commodity – or at least appear to save them time?**

  - **Friends – will it help the person be better known, build their network or gain access to a wider number of people?**

And know exactly when and how to push them.

6 **Be Certain.** To make any sale you have to ooze confidence, but not be arrogant. You have to be bold and humble. Being certain means generating awesome self-belief. Prove the faith in your own product or service by offering true risk-sharing, such as staged payments.

⑦ **Be Clever.** Make it easy to buy, and to evaluate once bought. Time is a cherished commodity, so don't take up too much of it. Make it absolutely clear what happens next, and make the process easy.

What happens when it goes wrong? How can you turn a lemon into a lemonade, and turn a customer around?

❶ *Take ownership – and decide that your customer will be delighted by the outcome.*
❷ *Remember, you have their attention, and you have the two ingredients you need for delicious 'lemonade' – their emotions are high, and their expectations of what you can deliver are low, rock bottom.*
❸ *Surprise them – do something that gobsmacks them, way over and way, way above what they thought you were capable of. It need not cost a lot; it may take time, but it will be worth it.*

They will talk about it with everyone they meet, and you will have a loyal customer for life.

If you wish to follow the chapters in the order they were written, please go to Chapter 2, on page 29.

enough is enough

Workplace bullying is alive and well and thriving in an organization near you – although hopefully not too close.

Bullying at school is bad enough, bullying at home is worse, but workplace bullying is in many ways the worst of all because it is ill defined, unexpected and your very livelihood depends on your compliance.

There is widespread controversy on the subject, with expert opinions sharply divided. At the one extreme, the last year has seen thousands come forward and claim that they had been the victims of bullying. Opponents claim it is people misreading normal professional behaviour, that business is a hard world anyway, and that many of these individuals are merely attention seeking, or playing victim.

Enough is enough.

So, first, in keeping with the spirit of this book, let's give it a definition, so we can all understand what we are talking about and have a chance of taking control of it.

What is bullying?
Whilst many people associate bullying with the playground, children who get away with bullying at school go on to be bullies in the workplace. So called 'Business Bullies' behave as they do to hide their personal or professional inadequacy. The more adequate the bully, the more extreme the bullying, the more determined is the bully to project his or her inadequacy onto others. In a poorly managed workplace, this is how incompetent people keep their jobs.

Bullying occurs when one person in a position of power tries to control or undermine another person using aggressive physical and/or psychological strategies, on a consistent basis. The term 'bully' describes a range of behaviours, from a persistent unwillingness to recognize performance, loyalty and achievement, to repeated critical remarks, to overtly hostile behaviour such as shouting at an employee in front of colleagues.

In short – if any other human being makes you feel unhappy, that is wrong. You have every right as both a human being and an employee to go about your work free of fear and intimidation.

Tim Field, one of the world's foremost experts on business bullying (check out *www.bullyonline.org*), cites the following circumstances for bullying to thrive:

- **Stress – this is becoming a major issue for all leaders.**

- **Speed of change.**

- **Not being valued in an organization.**

- **Long hours culture – working late still attracts serious brownie points in too many companies.**

- **Information overload.**

- **Pressure of work.**

- **Uncertainty – threats of redundancy and downsizing.**

What happens to the victim?

The target of bullying finds their work and relationships are sabotaged, information is withheld, leave and training are denied, and impossible objectives are set. An inevitable mistake is exploited as the basis for imposing disciplinary action or competency procedures. After a year or two of this behaviour, and after all attempts to resolve the conflict with dialogue have come to nought, the target of bullying finds themselves on sick leave, exhausted and with many of the symptoms resulting from prolonged negative stress.

Not only must leaders address these damaging cultural issues, they must constantly review their management styles to ensure they are not abusing their positions of power. And, when someone comes forward for help, leaders must lend a sympathetic and understanding ear.

Everyone has a right to carry out their work without being harassed, or having their self-confidence or self-esteem undermined.

Of course, the ultimate irony about bullies is that the

reason they attack your self-esteem, is because theirs is very low in the first place.

This may be down to personal feelings of inadequacy, or indeed down to professional jealousy. Bullies go into overdrive when they know they can't compete at a professional level, and may try all sorts of tricks.

One example I know of was when a bully went to a hard-working manager's boss and said he (the bully) was worried about the manager concerned, who 'seemed to be looking very pale, and stressed'. By doing this the bully gave the impression he cared and planted seeds of doubt about this manager's health (and therefore ability) in the mind of the person's boss, without giving away his true intentions!

What can I do about it?

The key to dealing with bullying is early recognition. Bullies excel at deception and manipulation, but betray themselves through recognizable patterns of behaviour and character traits which include a Jekyll and Hyde nature, compulsive lying, charm and an exceptional verbal facility.

Serial bullies exhibit a history of conflict with staff which manifests itself through high staff turnover, abnormal levels of sickness absence and unaddressed complaints from former employees – all of which can be recorded, measured and investigated.

In the absence of effective legislation, many employers are more scared of the serial bully than they are of the employees; only after the serial bully has left, will their incompetence, wrongdoings, maladministration and sometimes misappropriation of budgets become clear.

If you are being bullied, or you know someone who is, it may not be easy. However, you must stand up and do something about it. Go straight to Human Resources and tell them what is happening. Or confront the person concerned.

Many people find the whole subject of bullying incomprehensible, funny even. If that applies to you, ask yourself the following question before you put your head back in the sand:

'Have I seen anyone being treated unfairly, aggressively even, on a regular basis?'

If the answer to that is yes, do something about it, and do it now.

With thanks to Tim Field, author of *Bully in Sight*, *www.bullyonline.org*.

Stand Up and Be Counted

When Khrushchev pronounced his famous denunciation of Stalin, someone in the Congress Hall is reported to have shouted: 'Where were you, Comrade Khrushchev, when all these innocent people were being slaughtered?'

Khrushchev paused, looked around the hall, and said, 'Will the man who said that kindly stand up.'

Tension mounted in the hall. No-one moved.

Then Khrushchev said, 'Well, whoever you are, you have your answer now. I was in exactly the same position then as you are now.'

Various sources

If you wish to follow the chapters in the order they were written, please go to Chapter 4, on page 43.

THE NAKED LEADER EXPERIENCE

Inspiration 35

shall we dance?

Crossing fingers while shaking hands used to mean the agreement was worthless. For customers and suppliers these days it more probably means wishing for luck.

There is so much worry, fear and negativity surrounding customer/supplier relationships, that developing them into trusted partnerships becomes ever more difficult. At best, we tolerate each other, engaging in ongoing pleasantries as we go about our business, interspersed with warning shots across the bow – about cost, service or anything else we can think of. At worst, we are simply expecting things to go wrong, and, with weighty contract at the ready, threaten to pounce.

While it is easy to blame suppliers, it is not the complete picture. Many customers, desperate to resolve a business need, take products and services without knowing exactly what will be delivered – or whether it will bring any real benefit to their organization.

At all levels, the success of the relationship is as much dependent on communication at the coalface as it is on your relationship with the supplier's representative or leader.

The following specific actions not only reduce risk, but also help develop a trusted, strategic partnership:

Customers:

- Clearly define what role the supplier or product will play, and the measurable business benefit that will be gained for your organization.

- Do not attempt to screw your supplier into the ground during contract/price negotiations – you will pay for it later.

- Consider appointing a full-time supplier 'manager' whose role is to ensure relationships with all suppliers are working as agreed. This person will oversee an overall standard to live up to, a code of conduct that all suppliers must follow.

- Never openly criticize any supplier – resolve disputes in private.

- Do not allow lapses in service to drag on; deal with such issues immediately.

THE NAKED LEADER EXPERIENCE

- Reward supplier delivery by recommending them to other customers, giving them free publicity and involving them in decisions. Or pay early for excellent work.

Suppliers:

- Clearly define the benefits of what you are offering to do – the real customer value. Only accept full payment on delivery of these benefits. In effect, guarantee your work. That will show you mean business, and believe in your own abilities/product. Make sure you understand and are capable of delivering what is expected of you.

- Be honest when things go wrong. Not only will this win you respect, but every crisis is an opportunity to prove you really care and can take fast action.

- See everything from your customer's point of view.

- Do not make your customer too reliant on your product or services. It may seem attractive to 'tie them in' but it usually has the reverse effect of causing resentment. Let your delivery speak for itself, and then get out. Believe me, your customer will be on the phone again, wanting to use you again, rather than feeling they have to.

- Bring something extra to the table – an idea or innovation for the customer – it may be completely unrelated to the proposed service.

Sadly, trust and handshakes are not enough, and while contracts have their place (locked away out of sight) they are a last resort. When companies have to rely on contract wordings the relationship is, most likely, beyond repair.

Somewhere between the two extremes of litigation and mutual adulation lies the winning balance that not only avoids serious dispute, but also gives the exciting possibilities of ever closer alliance and opportunity for mutual benefit.

There is so much doom and gloom about customer/supplier relationships. Take a strong decision to put the negatives to one side, and focus on some positive actions that will take your relationship forward to new strength, heights and achievements.

'How can we best select suppliers in the first place?'

The G.O.L.D. supplier system focuses on the big relationship issues, and avoids many of the lower level scientific measurements.

G.O.L.D. stands for:

- **Goals:** sharing goals and shaping the future together turns an agreed alliance into a formidable force.

- **Openness:** the main value that turns supplier relationships into trusted partnerships.

- **Leading Edge:** how innovative and imaginative are they?

- **Delivery:** track record is one thing – what your supplier is doing right now is what really counts.

To find out how a potential supplier rates, ask these questions. There are no scorings, no graphs or benchmarks,

THE NAKED LEADER EXPERIENCE

just gut-feel and perception – two of the most often cited reasons for supplier/customer relationships to break down.

Questions to ask:

1 *Tell us about ourselves, who are we, what do we do and where we are going.*

How prepared are they? Do they really want this business?

2 *What is the biggest mistake you have ever made with a customer relationship?*

Look for a specific and honest example of a complete screw-up. Watch out for a stock interview answer such as, 'The biggest mistake I ever made was to assume our customer understood our business.'

3 *What one idea would transform our company?*

Give them no warning of this, ask them when they are presenting/in a meeting.

4 *How many customers have you lost in the last twelve months?*

Again, be suspicious if they say none.

5 *I would like to speak with one of your customers, how can I do that, please?*

If they are good, they will give you a list of customers and you choose which you phone, if they are not, they will give you a chosen name to call.

6 *Will you guarantee your work?*

A gold-dust question. Worry if they say 'no', worry more if they say 'yes' without qualification. No-one can truly guarantee the work on its own; there have to be guarantees on both sides.

Much has been written about supplier relationships, and there are many tomes available that list scores of consider-ations. In many ways some of our problems have been indicative of the complexities of the supplier relationships we create. Whether you take this method as a whole, in part or just in the spirit in which it is intended to work, it cuts out a lot of hassle, and focuses on the key areas to make your professional relationships a success, now and in the future.

⑦ How many customers in our sector do you have?

This is not just for credibility – it is also for future co-operation. More companies are now realizing the benefits of talking with, and sharing information with, rival companies.

By the way, here's a technique you can use at these meetings, to assess the total turnover (or whatever) of everyone present, without revealing any individual figure: start with the Chairman, who thinks up a number, adds their company's turnover to that number, and writes the second figure down on a piece of paper. Each company adds their figure to that number as a cumulative, always folding over the paper so that the next person sees only the latest total cumulated figure.

When the paper returns to the Chair they subtract their first made-up figure (which only they know) and announce the final figure.

In one simple exercise the whole group knows the total turnover (or whatever) in the room, without anyone *knowing anyone else's individual figure.*

By the way, this exercise can be used for many things – such as measuring morale in your team without any one person revealing their own personal level.

If you wish to follow the chapters in the order they were written, please go to Chapter 24, on page 201.

downsizing to greatness . . .

The global economic rollercoaster that we ride today means that all companies, whatever their size, will have to go through the redundancy process at some stage. There is no such thing as a job for life any more.

As a leader, how you maintain and re-establish trust, hold on to and revive your cultures and release the potential in your remaining people will depend on you, and how you:

- **Carry out the redundancies.**

- **Treat the people whose jobs are made redundant.**

- **Communicate with the 'survivors'.**

Let's look more closely at these important points:

How you carry out the redundancies

In the early Nineties many organizations had to save costs and downsize, and most of these are still paying the price for the way they did it. Those that hid behind the veneer of an 'initiative' such as business process re-engineering are now regretting their methods, while those that were honest with their people recovered fast.

We can be straight with people *and* inspire them in tough times. Such leadership is easy in the good times but all too rare when the going gets tough. Anyone can sail a ship when the seas are calm.

Once you know you have to lose people, how do you do it? There are two extremes here, the American Hire-and-fire Model where you find an envelope on your desk after lunch or, worse still, an email, and what I call the Union Model, where, to avoid industrial tribunals, everyone is asked to apply for their own jobs, with only the successful ones staying. This may seem fairer, but you and I both know it is a complete sham, as you will have already decided who is staying and going.

Even worse, with voluntary redundancy you are likely to lose the people you most want to keep, as they will take the money and be able to walk into another job. Indeed, it would be more realistic if news that a company was carrying out voluntary redundancy caused its share price to fall, not rise!

As ever, the best way is somewhere in between the speed of the first and the costs of the second. You will know who you want to keep, so let the others go, fairly and fast. Be honest and as open as you can, because you will be judged by . . .

How you treat the people whose jobs are to be made redundant

This will stay in the corporate memory of your people for many years. The key here is to convince the person that their *job* is being made redundant, not them as individuals. However, as a person they will still feel rejected, their self-worth, value and belief in themselves crushed by one experience – particularly if they have been in a 'secure' job for years.

Regardless of size, you have a legal, professional and social responsibility to help people who leave your company. And while money is important, it comes second to coaching and retraining.

If you do everything in the right way, you will stay in contact with those people who leave your organization. And, when times improve, it is these people who are the best people to recruit once again.

Also, ensure that people who leave your organization are not blamed for anything – I know a project manager who was made redundant and was then blamed for everything that went wrong for the next year! This kind of behaviour is totally unfair and can seriously damage a person's reputation and chances of re-employment.

Finally, remember that badly handled redundancies can be a public relations disaster. All of that investment you have made in Corporate and Social Responsibility, in your brand image and values, will turn to dust as your ex-employees tell everyone how appalling they were treated. It is simply not true that every redundant person condemns their previous employer, so give them no excuse to do so.

How you communicate with the 'survivors'

Now is the time to stand up and be counted. Your people judge and respect you based on three factors, in this order: who you are, what you do and, finally, what you say, so this is not the time for long boring speeches about going forward. This is the time for emotional leadership, for winning over their hearts, and you need to do it fast.

Why? Because your future depends on these people.

Be open and honest, let everyone know where they stand, share your dream and invite theirs. Listen to everyone, put innovation at the heart of everything you do, and reward your people through recognition, thanks and involvement.

Encourage people to talk – about how they feel now, how they are dealing with increased workloads, their hopes and fears.

Focus on the future, and restore fun into your workplace as fast as you can. Like so many answers, those that will help you recover after redundancies lie within your company, right now. When you have to face, and make, tough decisions, you have a choice. If you do what you have always done, you will get what you have always got. So if your last redundancy experience went badly wrong, do things differently. The key is to come from a place of trust and integrity. When you do this, and you truly value everyone involved, those that leave and those that stay, you are a true leader.

Being made redundant is one of the most devastating experiences that can happen to us. As well as taking away our livelihood and threatening our safety and stability, it is like being told we are without worth, that we have no further part to play.

Frances Cook spent thirteen years growing and building the UK's leading outplacement firm, Penna Sanders & Sidney, which is proud to have helped many thousands of people at all levels to bounce back from redundancy and achieve their personal goals. She is now a business mentor with Merryck & Co and sits on several advisory boards. Her advice:

Facing Redundancy

What if it is you that is facing redundancy? Leaders are rarely spared the redundancy experience these days. In the age of mergers, acquisition, streamlining and repositioning, big savings can be made by cutting at the top or bringing business units together under a single leader. You could be the loser.

Face redundancy as you would any other business challenge, use all the weapons in your considerable armoury . . .

● **Take time to assess your situation, understand your aims, your life and work goals, your unique skills. Consider all the options and think creatively.**

● **Don't rush into quick decisions.**

● **Bring in the best team to help you prepare your plan and achieve your goals. Get professional support if you can (career consultancy/outplacement) or enlist the help of friends, colleagues, family and your social and business network.**

● **Do not underestimate the willingness of others to help. Many have faced this scenario before you, or expect to face it in the future.**

Research your market and develop an effective marketing plan. This will present you as the best candidate for the job; convince the bank to support your new business set up; help raise venture capital for a buyout or convince others to support retraining or new directions.

Have courage and resilience as you would in your working life – this is just another different phase of it. It's not easy finding a new dream to live but you will if you follow the principles which have made you successful before.

If you wish to follow the chapters in the order they were written, please go to Chapter 30, on page 255.

murders and acquisitions

When I was a boy I used to love comics. My favourite was a boys' weekly called *Jag*. I read it from issue one for over a year. And then, one week, they announced some 'Exciting News' across the front page. My *Jag* was going to merge with another boys' comic, called *Tiger*, and together, the joined forces would be the best comic in the world!

WOW, I was so excited. I would get all of my *Jag* stories, AND *Tiger's* stories, for the same price.

But it didn't work out like that.

The following week my new comic arrived, it was now called *TIGER and JAG*, fair enough (rolls off the tongue better than the other way around), but some of my favourite stories were missing.

In the next few weeks the title stayed the same, and then

one week it arrived and it was called *Tiger and Jag*, and a few weeks later it was *TIGER and Jag*, and two weeks later the *Jag* disappeared completely.

That's murder for you, murders and acquisitions.

And don't they continue to grow in number and scale? And how the audience applauds . . .

- The City loves it – shares often rise.

- The chairmen shake hands and enjoy a glass of champagne.

- The press offices proclaim a true partnership based on vision, values and true combined value.

And inside both organizations: chaos. Because such developments bring uncertainty. On security, on jobs, on the future.

So how can two companies, two giants coming together, learn to truly dance, rather than collide?

The main risks are:

- Losing the very best people immediately to other jobs.

- Losing other good people as soon as voluntary redundancy is announced – because the first people who apply are those most able to find other positions, or start up on their own.

- Losing the hearts and minds of remaining employees during the entire process, putting at risk ongoing business.

● **Losing shareholder value because the joint benefits are rarely the sum of the two parts.**

Then there are the politics and the egos. No matter how many studies are carried out, or reports written, mergers inevitably mean an immediate power struggle, as the cake is divided up.

With acquisitions, the acquired company almost always ends up fighting for survival, and the acquirer is so often the winner – no matter what promises were made (the *Tiger and Jag* scenario).

Here are the actions to take to ensure the mines in this minefield are avoided, and that one plus one really is more than two:

● **Speed of decision.** End the uncertainties as soon as you can, particularly if there is duplication of departments or projects. Avoid, if you can, long drawn-out research and reports.

● **'Culture'.** Many people cite culture clashes as one of the reasons mergers do not work. What is culture if not people? So, it's up to your people to make it work – in particular those in middle-leadership or middle-management. These are the people who will feel most in the dark. They have their teams looking up to them to provide answers they do not have, and their own bosses not passing down all the information they need, usually because it is not available.

● **Openness.** Be as open as you can – and being open does not mean the occasional, carefully worded briefing. It means being visible like you have never been visible before. It means sharing anything and everything as soon as you can, and most of all it means making sure that everyone, every single human being, can come to you or know where to go to find something out, without fear or favour. If they do this, and you do not know the answer, promise that you will get back to them, and then make sure that you do!

- **Vision.** Never lose sight of why you have joined forces, and keep focused on that. Equally, the top leaders in an organization do not know all the answers, and must therefore openly seek help from their people.

- **Humility.** Nothing galls me more than seeing a 'victorious' company gloating over the spoils of a newly taken-over company. It does not have to be like that, and this kind of arrogance brings no credit to the perpetrators.

- **That said,** be careful of equal partnerships. Think carefully before you announce partnerships of equals, because while in the boardroom that may all look sweet, your people do not know what it means. In fact, it usually means there will be even more chaos and uncertainty throughout the organizations.

- **Technology.** Often the longest to sort and often also the area that can deliver most value. Involve your IT leaders early on.

In the twenty-first century, more companies will come together.

And of course, it is not companies coming together, it is people. Companies never change, people change. And it is up to the people to make it work.

The faster, more open and focused on the vision that you remain, the greater your chances of success, every time.

On the other hand, if you want to really screw up a merger or acquisition, do the following – you cannot go . . . right!

- **Have no clear idea of where you are going, then, when you don't get there, it doesn't matter.**

- **Ignore the people – who are they to have thoughts, concerns or contributions? Do this as early as possible so the best people leave first.**

- **Spend hours discussing things and never make a decision. Hold all meetings in secret.**

- **Treat everyone and everything that happens with suspicion. When that other company was a rival you knew where you stood, but now they are part of the same business family they cannot be trusted.**

If you wish to follow the chapters in the order they were written, please go to Chapter 33, on page 287.

IT's time to deliver

You've invested a lot of time, resources and money on your Information Technology. That's all the Systems, Software and Hardware that's cost you a small fortune, and from which you may not have had the returns you expected.

Before we bear down too hard on an industry that has provided me with my bread and butter for many years, there are many areas in which technology has transformed our lives, just ask companies such as EasyJet, First Direct or Amazon. And, of course, technology has delivered in so many areas – health, education, communication, etc.

The technology 'industry' is very young, and developing faster than many people, including me, can contemplate. There is more technology in your alarm clock than was used to put a man on the moon. Everything today seems smaller, faster and cheaper.

What about your organization?

I know only too well that IT is an easy target. Few understand what they do, they seem to spend money and sometimes their people seem to talk in a very strange language.

Has that knowledge management system really delivered value? What about data warehousing – all done and dusted? And how about customer relationship management – do they love you now?

The overall question that must be answered, by people inside IT and in other areas inside organizations, is this:

Is your IT department your Supplier of Choice? What I mean by this is: if you had an open choice between using your IT department or a competitive supplier, which would you choose?

So, turning to IT leaders, how can you transform your performance?

In one over-riding way:

Be business, first, last and always, which means:

● **Understand the business of your organization.**

● **Talk in a business language that your peers understand.**

● **Above all, never talk about what technology is, always talk about what technology can do – the results it can deliver.**

Business decision-makers don't care one hoot what the technology is, they want to know what it does. Some people call these killer applications, but it goes wider than this. It extends and grows when it comes to the Internet. As far as the majority of your customers are concerned, by the way, a 'cookie on your desktop' means a baked biscuit ready to eat, as opposed to a downloaded piece of software that causes Internet pop-ups.

You can also now buy software that automatically codes software, for example Java. Such applications are reducing project time scales by more than ten-fold. We have no excuses any more.

As an IT leader it's your choice. Be forever seen as a cost, a 'technology tool' and unwelcome, or be seen as an investment, a 'business enabler' and be loved by all.

And two ground rules:

- **Never, never – that's never – use the term 'user'. As Michael Meltzer told me once, there are only two industries that have that term: the IT industry and the drugs industry.**

- **There is no such thing as an 'IT project'. Everything is a business project, indeed, everything is a change project. Many companies have learnt this to their cost. The new IT system at British Airways check-in desks cost the company at least £40 million, because they did not manage the associate change properly.**

Here're my top ten ways to become your company's 'Supplier of Choice'.

1 Your Mission is Their Mission
Save a fortune on yellow Post-Its and wasted effort. As an IT department, your vision is your company's vision. If the overall corporate goal is to be the number-one car rental company, that must be your team's goal, as well.

2 Hidden Account Management (sometimes known as man-marking)

Put simply, identify the key decision-makers in your organization and allocate one of your people to each person. Your person's role is to ensure their allocated decision-maker catches IT doing something right on a consistent basis. This is the single most powerful method in transforming perception. (See *The Naked Leader* or download the chapter free at *www.nakedleader.com/ham*).

3 The Language You Use

IT has become riddled with jargon, so much so that attending some meetings with IT people is like taking a crash course in double-Dutch. It's time to speak plain business English in all that you do. If you have anyone who can't do this, keep them out of the way, preferably in a locked room. Clear, concise, compelling meanings, all day, every day.

4 Deliver, Deliver and Deliver

Prioritize all major projects (everything cannot be a number-one priority). Make sure that the benefits that people say will be delivered actually are, by ensuring a business leader takes responsibility for their delivery. Be specific, get a real figure and record it.

5 Leadership of Change

As an IT team, you are best placed in any organization to facilitate successful change. This does not mean that you should take control of change. It means that you must place yourself at the heart of the process; ensure that change happens effectively, by bringing all relevant people, teams and departments together. This also places you at the heart of your business, where you must be.

6 Take Ownership of Your Web Activities, and Prove Your Worth

Keep your website clear, simple and uncluttered. Also, install the latest customer-prediction management systems, enabling you to predict what your customers will do next. Watch out though, your marketing director will think you are after his or her job. (Which is clearly not true, because you will already have it.)

7 Introduce Project Leadership

One of the hottest topics around. Forget traditional and boring project management, put your projects in the hands of inspiring communicators, who are action driven and who keep their heads while all around are losing theirs. And learn lessons from those projects that *don't* go well, and those that do.

8 Talk Yourself Up (internal)

Celebrate successes, enjoy what you are doing. Change the culture and encourage the individuality of your people within the framework of the team. If you don't think you are delivering outstanding results, no-one else will.

9 Location

Are you still behind three armour-plated doors that would not look out of place in a jeweller's shop? If you are, get out fast! IT suppliers of choice are located close to other departments in an organization.

10 Recruit People from Outside the IT Industry

Recruit people with a broad range of skills. More IT leaders are being recruited and promoted from non-technical backgrounds, and as communication and relationship building are two of the top skills for IT departments who are suppliers of choice, such 'soft' (read 'critical') skills are much needed.

In the early Nineties, partly as a result of so many companies reeling from the disasters caused by downsizing, whole areas of technical support were outsourced. Some high-profile deals were signed for ten years plus. Now many companies are pulling these areas back in-house, realizing that in tomorrow's IT world, infrastructure and its associated skills are business critical.

The latest buzz is to outsource applications development, with whole areas of project teams and development being passed over to third parties.

This push-me-pull-you approach is simply not working. It may be good news for the legal departments; it is not good news for IT departments, or the companies that depend on them.

The successful IT department of the future will focus on *best sourcing*. In doing this they will ask three questions, and adopt three roles:

- **What is best for my company? (Business Broker)**

- **Who will bring about the most effective change, fastest? (Change Enabler)**

- **What skills do I need to keep in-house, to ensure I can keep control? (Human Resources)**

And, for the whole organization:

Incredible as it may seem, more information technology (IT) development takes place outside corporate IT departments, than within. The growing PC population and an increasing number of 'power users' have created an enormous and mission-threatening challenge to too many organizations.

This is how it happens.

Disenchanted with the out-of-date online applications, and not understanding the IT project process, people go ahead and develop their own local solution, to meet their particular needs.

They are very proud of this, and soon pass it round the department, and the company, so that more people can use it.

It quickly becomes a strategic application, being enhanced all the time.

'So what?' you may ask. We supply the machines, the easy-to-use applications, and if business people choose to develop their own solutions, that is relieving the burden from IT departments. Also, PCs are integral to many people's work.

These are compelling arguments. However, such developments rarely have any documentation, so the original developer quickly becomes the local help desk, which is fine until they leave the department or company, or it becomes too much for them.

Such developments seldom follow any standards or procedures. Ownership is unclear – until something goes wrong, when IT own it, even if this is the first they have heard of the application (what a lame excuse!)

Business people start to spend more time playing with applications than doing the job for which they were employed. And putting such applications on local area networks – as is often requested – can bring down other systems.

Word quickly spreads that IT is slow at doing things, compared with Mike in Marketing who will run you off an Excel macro in two days. Mike then becomes his own IT service department, and doesn't he love it!

The hidden costs associated with this trend are enormous. These applications must be explained, supported and even integrated with existing systems.

Never, that is NEVER, change a software package.

The moment you do, it is no longer a package. Now, many of you will shout a big NO when you read the next sentence. However, please let us remember, if we do what we have always done, we will get what we have always got:

> Fit your business to the software package, not the other way around.

It's the only way packages will work. Your competitive advantage comes from the additional activities and information you get from the package, not by changing the package itself.

Standardize on one office suite (word processor/ spreadsheet, etc) throughout your company.

Trust me, and save a fortune.

The arguments for standardization are many:

- Transformed improvement in the IT department's ability to resolve problems – as the support staff will not have to deal with many different configurations.

- More time can be spent addressing the people side – such as additional training.

- Faster installation of PCs.

- Trainees become productive more quickly as they have less to learn.

- Clearer set of skills needed for training.

- More effective monitoring of network activity – increasing prevention, and reducing problems.

- Saved business time and frustration as one or two people resolve the problem, instead of the previous dozen who used to come and go.

There is no such thing as free software.

All companies selling software are in it to make money. The pioneers of open-source are now very upset that what was deemed to be free and available to all, is lining people's pockets.

Be aware, be very aware . . .

Ten Things to Know about the Internet and Email

1 *It is not good or evil, everything depends on how it is used.*
The Internet's purpose used to be about seeking information

and acquiring knowledge, now it is about connecting people, everything else is just functional.

Thomas Power
Chairman of Ecademy

② **You cannot get a virus from reading an email, they sit in attachments.** If your attachments open automatically, you are at risk. If you are unsure about an attachment, reply asking the person if they sent it to you intentionally, and install security.

③ **Hoaxes are amongst the most dangerous types of virus.** Beware of any email that tells you to delete a file from within your computer system, chances are you need it. If you receive such an email, check out a security site before you do anything or you may regret it later.

④ **Never give out your real name or any personal details in chat rooms.**

⑤ **For your children. If anything happens in a chat room – or by email – that disturbs you or makes you feel uncomfortable, tell your parents or a trusted friend. Don't simply ignore it.**

⑥ **Microsoft will not give you money to forward a Microsoft email and neither will any other company.**

⑦ **Chain letters will not cause you any harm.** If you want to send on ten copies, send them all to me at *chainmail@nakedleader.com*. In the last year, I have received over 10,000 from people, not sent any on, and I am still alive and well.

8   **NEVER, NEVER, NEVER reply or write to a spammer (some-one who sends you spam mail) asking to be removed from its list.** NEVER click the 'click here to remove your name' box. All that does is confirm that they have found an active account. Instead, delete the email.

9   *If you write an email from the office, remember your employer has the legal right to look at anything and everything you send or receive.*

10 **Never put anything on your hard drive (the permanent part of your computer software) that you wouldn't want the police to read.** There is no such thing as privacy in cyber-space and there is no such thing as a deleted file. A good cyber detective can recover almost anything.

With thanks to The Everything Tall Tales, Legends, and Outrageous Lies Book
By Nat Segaloff

If you wish to follow the chapters in the order they were written, please go to Chapter 26, on page 217.

ten white manuals . . .

A man wanders into a trophy shop.
Gosh, he thinks, looking around. This guy must be good.

Picture the scene: you have just finished a leadership
course and you are on a HIGH. The final action was to
share your new ambitions and dreams with your
colleagues, and then it was a bit of bonding in the bar
followed by a euphoric drive home.

Euphoric, because:

* **You know you are unstoppable.**

* **You have had a five-day break from work, so you feel
refreshed and ready for anything.**

- **You now have the tools and techniques to catch anything that is thrown at you.**

You arrive home, and share your experiences with your partner – you tell the funny stories, prolonging the one where a certain colleague who will remain nameless – know who I mean? – got really drunk on the first night, and embarrassed himself and everyone around him. You don't have time to cover the story about how you were equally legless on the second night.

On Monday morning, you wake up early, and go straight into work. You place the manual on your desk, and set to work:

- **Visioning.**

- **Planning.**

- **Dreaming how things will be different.**

You notice the HR manager coming in. You rush out, and share your experiences with him. He seems very pleased for you but points out that while you were away on this 'jolly' they had hit some serious problems. Also, one of his staff has resigned, and he finishes off by saying: 'Still, mate, really pleased you enjoyed it, can't wait to hear more about it. But if you don't mind some of us have got some *real* work to do.'

Oh well, you think, he's just jealous.

On your way back to your desk, you glance up at the top shelf. There, sitting neatly side by side, are all of the training manuals you have collected over the years.

This company has invested a great deal in your training,

and boy have you repaid it. Well, you'd like to, if only the people who sent you on these courses actually valued what you learnt and brought back to 'base'.

Then your PA arrives, more colleagues come in, and slowly the day, the routine, takes over . . .

At the end of the day you lift up the manual and place it alongside the other six on the top shelf.

There were six on the shelf and the little one said, 'Move over, move over.'

And they all moved over and the seventh one joined . . .

It simply doesn't have to be like that.

Blank page intended
(As it says in so many training manuals.
Why? To draw on?)

You can take a person to the seminar, but you can't make them learn.

Adrian Gilpin
Institute of Human Development

There is another way.

For years we have been grappling with training – always our company's number-one priority, and always the first to be cut from the budgets. We hide training under any other topic we can, as it is very important to keep our people's skills up to date . . .

And leadership training, well, that is all the rage. We must turn all of our managers into leaders, must develop the next generation, must . . .

And year after year, we continue to send people on course after course.

Question – does it have a massive, positive impact on our organizations?

When we return from our courses, does the company receive a bottom-line return?

All too rarely.

There were seven on the shelf and the little one said, 'Move over, move over.'
And they all moved over and the eighth one joined . . .

Why?

- **Is it because the quality of training is poor? No.**

- **Is it because some people are incapable of learning new skills? No, they may choose not to, but they are more than capable.**

- **Is it because you don't have catch-ups and refresher days? No, they operate in abundance.**

It is because people going on such courses do not make even one true decision *during the course itself*.

Remember, a true decision is one in which you attach yourself to a dream/outcome and you close off any other possibility. It's powerful stuff, also painfully rare in leadership training.

And how long does it take to make such a decision?

A single heartbeat.

And your heart will beat many times when you are on the course. And if you have made a true decision yourself, to do one thing differently, no matter what happens on your return, your heart begins to dance.

And if your training has focused on team-building, and you have all made the collective decision to work closely together, as one unstoppable team, your hearts will feel as if they are beating in unison.

And if you decide to take your company to new heights, and you close off all other options, you will have the passion to get other heartbeats soaring when you return.

There were eight on the shelf and the little one said, 'Move over, move over.'
And they all moved over and the ninth one joined . . .

You notice the HR manager coming in. You rush out and share your experiences with him. He seems very pleased for you but points out that while you were away on this 'jolly' they had hit some serious problems. Also, one of his staff has resigned, and he finishes off by saying: 'Still, mate, really pleased you enjoyed it, can't wait to hear

THE NAKED LEADER EXPERIENCE

more about it. But if you don't mind some of us have got some *real* work to do.'

You smile to yourself, how predictable is that? Not very! This time things will be different. This time you say, 'Gerry, I have made some decisions about myself and have some proposals for the company which I believe will give us the breakthrough we need. Now, Gerry, you're a visionary, let's talk these through and then we can go have a chat with the Board.'

You are in persuasive mode, not in post-training-blues mode.

Next time you design or deliver a course, next time you are on a course, make sure time is allocated for you and others to make and take away a true decision.

With training, you don't have to believe everything you are told and taught. You just decide to do something about it – and you do this during the course.

Then the manuals can sit on your shelves with pride. Now you will actually refer to them, and read them again, to support how you will make your decision happen. And now, they will feel important.

There were nine on the shelf and the little one said, 'Move over, move over.'
And they all moved over and the tenth one joined.
And then the shelf collapsed.

Nasrudin was very clear on what 'success' meant in his sky-diving training course.
'How many sky dives do I have to complete successfully?' said a hopeful aspirant to the school.
'All of them,' said Mulla.

Thanks to Bill Parslow

If you wish to follow the chapters in the order they were written, please go to Chapter 5, on page 49.

THE NAKED LEADER EXPERIENCE

over the Cs

The first few years of the third millennium will be remembered as the coming of the Cs. They are all over the place, not just on newly printed business cards. There are conferences, academic papers and writings galore.

We have CEO, COO, CFO, CIO, CTO, CKO and even CCO!

The C and O remain the same – C for Chief, O for Officer. It's the middle name that counts for everything!

In the above list, for example, we have Executive, Operating, Financial, Information, Technology, Knowledge and Change (I have also heard a CCO as being a Chief Communications Officer).

What do they all do?

CEO – Managing Director, the person in charge, probably.

COO – The guy that does all the work, day to day, and takes the blame for everything.

CFO – Posh new name for Financial Directors, same job as it always was.

CIO – New name for IT Director – to some it stands for Career is Over! (The sad thing is that IT directors invented this joke!)

CTO – A technology home for technology people who can be happy at last.

CKO – A meaningless title. If you are called this watch out – you are effectively on sabbatical!

CCO – If this means Change be warned – no one person can be held responsible for all change in any company. If this means Communications be even more warned, no one person can be accountable for all communications. In either case, watch your back!

OK, so the titles do not matter.

Let's move beyond titles.

What are the new, key roles that will be in demand in the next few years?

The Interim Manager (IM)

Your director has resigned, and it looks like it will take several months to find a replacement. Perhaps your company wants to look at the overall role and its future, or to evaluate the internal staff that, with the right development, could fulfil it. The IM specializes in holding the fort. They oversee day-to-day operations until a long-term plan is in place. Many people are choosing this role, as it offers many challenges, and an opportunity to learn while working in different companies.

Key skill: fast-track learning.

The Cultural Transformer (CT)

Their first priority is the motivation of staff, the release of human potential, and the destruction of hierarchies. Taken to an extreme, this person will actively encourage chaos, providing it enables people, ideas and action to thrive. The CT is visionary, energetic and visible, and thrives in a post-downsizing environment. Be careful though, they will want to change everything they touch.

Key skill: the ability to inspire.

The Turnaround King (TK)

The company is in trouble. Perhaps key projects are off track, costs are soaring and customers are deserting. The TK specializes in repositioning projects, teams and departments. The role is far from negative – he or she can be a saviour and is much more preferable than the receivers.

Key skill: bags of courage.

The Project Deliverer (PD)

The PD delivers, time and again. Specializing in the consistent completion of projects and major tasks on time, to budget and meeting business needs. Fast becoming a rare breed, the PD will also put in place a process and approach that will ensure projects bring real value to their organization. Project leadership at its best.

Key skill: persistence to deliver, against all odds.

The Master of Change (MC)

Although not to be recommended, many organizations are taking on Change Directors. So if it's a role in demand and you fancy a shot . . . The business is change, and of course you will know that the way to achieve this is through choice.

The successful MC places themselves at the heart of an organization, not 'leading' change, rather 'facilitating' it. It is a horizontal role rather than a vertical one, running through all business areas.

Key skills: business vision.

Although everyone will practise different approaches as the needs demand, people will have a favourite and dominant style. The ideal, of course, would be to have a mix – with at least one of each in your top team.

No matter which of these you feel you specialize in, there are some catch-all skills that are in huge demand, across all of the Cs.

Cathy Holley, one of the country's leading headhunters, is on a mission to strip away the hype and mystery, and reveal the truth about headhunting.

Here are her top seven tips for being headhunted:

1. *Be visible – that means working in well-respected companies. I will not be hunting in second-rate organizations; my clients do not want me to present candidates from them and rarely consider candidates from 'independent consultants'.*

2. *Be outstanding at what you do and leverage your success. Be your own best PR. Speak at public events, be quoted in trade/national press – be the industry expert and the one people consult. Reputation is key.*

3. *Be well regarded (not necessarily liked) by everyone you come into contact with. Don't make enemies. I may use your colleagues or employees as a source and may even*

take notice of what your former PA says about how you conduct yourself.

4 *Be easy to identify – have a sensible title ('VP' does not help me at all), be prominent on the web/annual report. Make sure the trail leads to your door!*

5 *Prime your PA not to filter out headhunter calls. He/she should be working for you, not your organization.*

6 *Come and find us! If we can't find you and don't know you, we can't headhunt you. Do you know who the top head-hunters are in your space? If you don't know them, they almost certainly don't know you. Call them up and intro-duce yourself – you then have thirty seconds to make the right impression. Be a friend and give help and information when it is needed (you scratch my back . . .). Feed them industry gossip.*

7 *Once you have been approached there is still a long way to go; you still have to impress the headhunter. This is a buyers' market (i.e. client, not candidate driven) and as BA would say, never forget we 'have a choice'. Invest in your own personal brand and be prepared to differentiate yourself.*

If you wish to follow the chapters in the order they were written, please go to Chapter 27, on page 225.

the next business greats

Make no little plans; they have no magic to stir man's blood.
Daniel Burnham

There is a new business age coming. A commercial, global and personal vision that puts:

Cause over Cash
Clarity over Confusion
Choice over Change

Cause over Cash

What is the mission, the aim, the dream of your organization? How closely aligned are these stated aims, with the aims of your people?

What does your organization do to make this world a better place to live in, for all its people?

Corporate and Social Responsibility (CSR) are at the forefront of the agenda for the New Business Greats who realize that when they get their cause – their mission, their purpose – right, it delights customers, who now care deeply about these issues, and if they delight customers, they make more cash.

Every major organization now has a policy and statement on CSR. However it is not enough to merely talk about it. Action is all. With CSR, words are cheap.

And CSR goes to the very heart of an organization – into the boardroom. Trust is very high on customers' and shareholders' agendas. Most leaders are trustworthy, but there are too many who are not. Organizations that place integrity high on their agendas know they must be more open and honest, and that their leaders cannot be rewarded for failure with massive pay-offs.

If Naked Leadership is about one overriding thing inside organizations, it is about trust, values and integrity.

Clarity over Confusion

It is time for radical simplicity inside our organizations. Many have over-processed themselves into chaos, with too many projects happening at the same time, and with such a focus on muddled detail that everyone seems to have forgotten the destination.

Make your dream clear, concise and compelling, and live it, inside and out, every day.

Choice over Change

The change agenda is dead – long live the choice agenda, because when people make choices, they, their teams and their companies transform faster than through any single change initiative.

Your Future – Your Chance

Regardless of economic conditions, challenges and constraints, future success can be yours. Indeed, the future presents matchless opportunities for liberation, success and achievement.

The future is a huge, compelling vision full of unlimited possibilities, wonderful excitement and massive rewards. At least it is for those prepared to see it. The majority of organizations and their people are so much more than what they have become.

Business leaders can see, embrace and celebrate this new, transformational agenda, leading their companies and people on an adventure to forge a new, compelling and exciting future. Or they can bemoan their circumstances, see only problems and be frozen into inaction, fear and uncertainty.

In this first decade of the third millennium, four 'realities' are combining to make this time a turning point in global business.

Reality One

The pace for change that started in the late Eighties, gathering momentum through the Nineties has now become all pervasive. It has taken many traditional and newer companies by surprise, and those that have failed to react have suffered, with many going out of business or being taken over. There is now an urgent need to be fast, fit and flexible – to focus on massive action and achievement. In this environment, the wrong decisions will be the slow ones.

Reality Two

In the last two years of the twentieth century, it seemed that technology overtook our imagination. For the first time in our history, whatever we wished to do in business and in life, the technology was available to enable us to do it. This means that all companies must change priorities to focus on the release of human ideas, imagination and insight.

Reality Three

The third reality is a growing disillusionment with the traditional approaches to consultancy, in particular, with the culture of dependency that traditional consultancy has encouraged. I call this the *Deadly Embrace*.

No longer can one company provide all of the answers – long-term transformation will come from services being offered by a mix of companies. In addition, it is now obvious that traditional 'off the shelf formula' management-consultancy answers have not helped companies to soar into the twenty-first century.

This can easily be resolved, when consultancies and consultants help their clients to do what they (the consultants) do. This is self-sufficiency, this is freedom, and it is the only way forward.

By doing this, and by helping clients to set up their own, internal consultancies, the reputation, image and delivery of consultancy will be transformed.

Is it commercial suicide?

THE NAKED LEADER EXPERIENCE

Of course not – quite the reverse, because people will want to use their services for updates, rather than feel they have to. Remember: we hate to be sold to, we love to buy.

And so I say this to all consultancies out there: the only way to control your clients is to set them free.

Reality Four

Finally, in the last decade of the twentieth century global corporations invested literally billions of global currency in initiatives. And they seemed to breed like rabbits. You would come back from holiday and discover yet another initiative – oh joy!

As one Chief Executive told me: *With Business Process Re-engineering, companies tended merely to re-engineer the processes they were already doing.*

You would think we had learnt, but at the time of writing one of the latest fads is Business Decision Re-engineering, which looks to me like BPR with a clown's hat on.

My advice, when it comes to any initiatives:

- **Ideas that come from within can be of far greater value than those imposed from outside. Create a culture where ideas can be freely expressed without blame or ridicule.**

- **Focus on addressing the big issues around customer retention, service and acquisition – don't get bogged down in the drink machine location trivia.**

- **Beware company and industry initiatives that try to be all things to all people – it is how it will work in *your* department that counts.**

- **There are ways of reducing numbers or instigating perceived negative change without hiding behind a false premise. People are not stupid.**

- **Talk about the initiative in a language that everyone will understand.**

- **Reward innovation and ideas through recognition and monetary payments.**

- **Emphasize the positive – growth and moving forward – not hunting out mistakes or penny pinching.**

And, most important of all:

- **Any and all company-wide initiatives should be subject to the same cost v benefit analysis as other projects and not just pushed to the top of the priority list by default.**

Next time such an initiative hits your company or department, ensure it is prioritized and treated like all other project requests. Ask the same basic business questions that accompany any strategic request. What are the costs, time scales and benefits?

If there are more questions and uncertainty than answers and direction ask the initiative's sponsor 'why are we doing this?' If the response is long and full of jargon, then start clearing some space on your shelves.

It's out of control, and it's coming your way.

And please, whatever you do, or whatever you call it, make it interesting:

Picture the scene – you are sitting in your dentist's chair.
He is staring into your mouth, justifying why he is about
to inflict serious pain. You look around, vainly hoping for
something to look at other than the teddy bear poster on
the ceiling.

Just as he is about to drill, he stops, smiles and offers you
a choice.

'I can either drill deeper into that cavity or give you this
Total Quality Management manual to read – your choice.'

'DRILL, DRILL', you scream.

These four realities are the cornerstones of business learning from the last twenty years. The momentum of change, technology overtaking imagination, the failure of traditional consultancy to prepare companies for the future and the focus on process above people provide us with valuable experience, insights and lessons on how to succeed in the future.

The past and the future are best witnessed through energy, enthusiasm and excitement. Have a deep, honest look at your organization today. Do you have these?

Be all that you already are.

You are capable of achieving anything you wish, and more.

Already inside your organization you have all the energy, innovation and knowledge that you need. Look up – there it is, walking around.

When people awaken their potential, their imaginations and their energies, the results are astounding. And it can happen to anyone, any team, any company. Any one person, group of people or organization that has ever experienced success, even just once, is capable of achieving that same success, at any time. Once you embrace this idea and put it into action, you hold in your hands a power that is quite awesome.

Many people will encourage you to be more than you have become.

Many companies will say they can help you to be the very best that you can be.

I invite you, as an individual, a team or a company, to be the very best that you already are.

People and Passion over Process and Procedure

We are entering a period that is the antithesis to the business process re-engineering mentality that wasted so many millions, destroyed the trust between company and employee, and enabled so many companies to, at best, stand completely still.

It is time for technology to come of age, it is time to reawaken a human spirit that has been dormant for far too long, and it is time to combine these two awesome powers for the benefit of all – your people, your shareholders, your organization. I say this to all leaders who are ready to achieve a level of success they had previously never dreamt possible, stand up – your time has come.

A time when we take back control of our own destinies, when we reawaken a human passion that has been dormant for too long and when those who choose success will be installed as the New Greats of this third millennium.

And when does this next business age begin?

Whenever you so choose.

Georgina Woudstra and Allard de Jong are two of the lead-ing coaches in the world. They argue that yesterday's leadership concepts are failing us. Our immediate future calls for leaders that are able to inspire a grander vision of the world we all live in. A world that is very different from today's world. New Leaders know that dreams can become reality. New Leaders open our eyes and lift our spirits. They see people's amazing, unique talents and pure potential, and their desire is to give people back to themselves.

They take this one stage further, arguing that to achieve this, leaders and organizations need rely on no-one other than themselves. Their approach, to transfer coaching skills as well as knowledge into a team and people within that team, so those people can fly by their own wings, is total reinvention of coaching throughout the world.

If you wish to follow the chapters in the order they were written, please go to Chapter 9, on page 79.

welcome home

Every child is born a genius. 9,999 out of every 10,000 are
swiftly, inadvertently, de-geniused by grown-ups.
R. Buckminster Fuller

Think of the power of words, their force on ourselves and on others. When words happen, everyone rushes to put meaning on the words being used, and different people end up with different meanings, and therefore different realities. Sadly, our first interpretations of communications can often be negative. This is because our conscious mind is always looking to give everything a reason, a definition that is clear.

And when we look at a meaning, we search our experience (what we have lived through) and our knowledge (what we have learned), and what we don't find there we substitute for with our imagination.

Our conscious mind, with all of its analysis and need for reason, is a huge barrier to messages reaching our subconscious mind, where our true strengths, abilities and unlimited potential sit, waiting to be released or remembered.

> *Deep within man dwell those slumbering powers; powers that would astonish him, that he never dreamt of possessing; forces that would revolutionize his life if aroused and put into action.*
> Orison Swett Marden

Words, ideas and language can change people's lives. In my research for the *Naked Leader* books, I have discovered many amazing ways of relaxing, influencing and helping other people.

Is it possible to awaken some of the powers of our subconscious through the power of words?

Absolutely.

And where better to do it, than in Chapter 42. So many of you wanted this book to end on Chapter 42, like its predecessor.

And it has, if you are reading this from front to back.

So, with massive thanks to Igor Ledochowski, please keep an open mind as you follow, and I hope enjoy, the following.

When I sign copies of *The Naked Leader*, I often tell people that it is their book, and not mine.

They sometimes look very confused.

But I mean it.

This book, and its messages, is as much yours, as mine.

Because, although we have never met, I feel we know each other.

And as you continue to read this, you may go along with this idea, or you may not, or you may just go with the flow.

While you are sitting, reading these words, you may feel it is as if I am talking directly to you, and no-one else.

That it is just you and I.

It is as if you can hear my voice, can see my face, and can read my thoughts.

We find we have a connection together that is beyond these words and these pages.

If you enjoy ideas that can change your life, and you have read this in exactly the way that you have chosen, you will have gone through the same experience I went through in writing it.

Not necessarily exactly the same journey, just the same experience.

Because however you have read it, and however I have written it, we have both arrived at this same point, together.

You may have agreed with some of the ideas I have written, while not agreeing with others, and that shows what an open mind you have – open to the power, potential and possibilities that are inside you right now.

When we present new ideas to each other, we sometimes put up mental 'barriers'. Can you remember what it feels like to share your ideas with other people? Do you recall a feeling of whether people will agree with you?

Now, do you remember a moment when you really connected with someone, with your ideas? And as you did so, how the barriers came down?

As you trusted someone.
As you decided to pay them total and absolute attention.
As you really listened to what they were saying.
With a completely open mind.
Without making any judgements.
With your total awareness.
With your total everything.

How the barriers came down, without effort, easily and automatically.

And suddenly, you and they communicated with each other at a very deep, personal and trusted level.

And as you go back in time to feel how amazing and humbling that feeling was.

And as time moves forward, and these thoughts sink deep into your mind, you may find similar feelings of trust enter your mind.

They may be slight or they may be deep, whatever you are feeling right now is fine, and you find yourself allowing them to happen, and enjoying the experience.

As you go forward.

As you read on.

As you go with the flow that is starting to make you feel very relaxed, calm and centred.

And as you feel whatever you are feeling, and as you relax to whatever degree you are relaxing, it is as if the words on this page are becoming very clear to you, as if the book is moving closer to your eyes.

As if these words and you are connecting at a very deep level.

And I am speaking directly to your subconscious mind. Directly, to the real you.

You that is living, breathing and full of strength.

Privately, to the you that is reading these words, and feeling what you are feeling, as your true and amazing abilities, talent and potential become clear to you, right now.

And you are a human being.

A human *being*.

So, just . . .

Be.

Be You.

You feel what you feel.

You know what you know.

You are who you are.

And as you *are*, you find your breathing automatically deepens your relaxation.

As you breathe in, you breathe in energy and strength and a warm feeling that runs through your entire body, crossing into your mind and spirit.

And it feels very very calming.

And that's fine.

You may be more relaxed, you may find yourself breathing more slowly, or you may simply feel a warm glow of energy running through your whole body.

Or you may simply feel calm.

As your mind relaxes, and your breathing is deeper, you may feel new levels of energy, strength and belief flow through you.

Each and every word suggests these unique talents closer to the surface, as you feel at one with yourself, the world and everyone in it.

You are reading this book and these words.

Only you are reading this book and these words.

And it is very private, and it is wonderful.

Because it is the real you that is connecting with these ideas, connecting with these feelings, connecting with the real, authentic you.

The you that was born with unlimited potential.

The you, today, who still has all of that potential, plus all of the knowledge you have learnt and the experiences you have had.

It all adds up to an awesome, amazing person.

It all adds up to you.

It might be that some of your childhood dreams are returning to you.

It might be that you are remembering what it felt like to be unstoppable.

Or it might simply be that you now realize what a unique, special and gifted person you really are, and always have been.

And as you remember whatever you remember, and whether your dreams are clear to you, or they are not, you may find yourself realizing:

This is it – this is what it has all been about, and now I get it:

What lies before me.
And what lies behind me . . .
Are but blades of grass to what lies within me.

And whether your dreams are clear to you, or not, you know, and always will know, that you have everything you need to be anything you want.

And you have it right now.

You are an amazing person, an incredible human being, with gifts, talents and strengths beyond your wildest imagination.

Take that thought, and all of the warmth, and double them.

Now double them again . . .

And again.

And as you do, you may find these amazing deep feelings of wonder, of warmth and new strength flow through your body towards your very heart.

It is unstoppable, and so are you.

You always have been . . .

In all that is . . .
And all that was . . .

And all that will be.

And now, as you begin to realize your true self, and what you are really capable of, you begin to remember.

You remember who you really are.

You remember your first breath on this earth – the energy, powers and potential that breath held.

And it may seem like a long time ago, or it may feel it is just a moment ago, or it may be right now.

Because inside each and every one of us is something we were born with, that is ours and ours alone. It cannot be taught to you, or learnt by you.

It is something you remember.

A strength, a gift, a talent that was given to you when you came into this world.

And as you think back, and remember whatever you remember, you connect with the real, authentic you.

We spend so much time looking outside of ourselves, for what has always been within . . .

A power, an energy, and awesome unique talent, is already within you, waiting . . .

To help you achieve your dreams . . .

To help you to help others, close to you, or in need of your help . . .

To help you, to help make this world a better place to live.

It is time to live your life, the life that only you were meant to live.

And as you do so, you rejoice.

Privately, deep within yourself, you feel your dreams, your peace, your life, awakening like giants within you.

Dreams you know you can achieve – and help others to achieve.

An inner peace that is so deep and so still, it connects your very mind, body and spirit.

A life that is full of amazing possibilities, which you are now beginning to realize.

And as you finish this chapter, and put this book down, look around you, at the world, in this moment.

And smile, deep inside . . .

Because you know:

It is time.

It is time to remember who you really are.

It is time to reclaim your birthright.

Welcome home. It is time to return to your self.

We shall not cease from exploration
And the end of our exploring
Will be to arrive where we started
And know the place for the first time
T.S. Eliot

If you wish to follow the chapters in the order they were written, please go to Chapter 22, on page 183.

The Naked Leader Experience
The Author's Journey

David wrote the book in this order:

THE NAKED LEADER EXPERIENCE

DAVID TAYLOR has a 25-year track record with a number of major organizations, including Rolls-Royce, Hoechst and Cornhill, and acts as personal adviser to chief executives, golfers and leaders from all walks of life

He designs and delivers breakthrough leadership events internationally, is President of Certus, the Association of IT Directors, a faculty member of the Young Presidents' Organization, and an Associate Partner with the Ashridge Business School.

www.nakedleader.com.

Coming Soon – the final part of
The Naked Leader Trilogy:
The Naked Leader Adventure
Find Your Self in a Book
Written by David Taylor, and by You

You have decided it is time to discover who you really are, why you are here and what difference you can make in this world.

Travel on a journey of your own making, choosing which doors to open, which people to trust and which decisions to make, in this true choose-your-own-adventure for adults.

Encounter love, fear and your ultimate destiny as you meet and journey with real characters from your past, your present and your future.

Every time you read it, it will be different – unique, personal and truly interactive. Your book, your journey and your life.

Please visit David at *www.nakedleader.com* for exclusive advance extracts, to find out more about being a Naked Leader and to join the biggest social and aspirational network in the world.

index

THE NAKED LEADER EXPERIENCE

notes

notes

notes

notes

notes

notes

THE NAKED LEADER
By David Taylor

An illuminating and inspiring guide to unlimited success
'The *One Minute Manager* for a new generation'
Nigel Risner, co-author of *Chicken Soup for the UK Soul*

Imagine if you simply could not fail. What would you do?
Where would you go? Who would you be?

In *The Naked Leader*, David Taylor strips away the myth
and mystery, the jargon and hype to make personal and
professional success no longer a matter of chance but rather
a matter of choice.

Here, as David invites you to join him on an amazing
journey of adventure and discovery to a world of unlimited
opportunity, he reveals *the* single formula for guaranteed
success and shows you exactly how to:

- **Abandon doubts and uncertainty –**
assured success is available to *you* – right now!

- **Build deep and lasting relationships**
for fast track personal, team and business performance

- **Ignite the power of transformation**
to shape the future for you and your organization

However daunting the challenges you face, and wherever
you may be on the ladder to success, *The Naked Leader* is a
powerhouse of inspiration – and *your* passport to a world of
infinite possibilities.

'The business-book bestseller executives are taking on holiday'
Financial Times

A Bantam Paperback

0 553 81565 2